BLOOMING THROUGH CHAOTIC TIMES

ENDORSEMENTS

This book illuminates the complexity of human experiences and how best to navigate outcomes, especially the hard ones. The book charges us to look to the past to ask the difficult questions about human-living in this present decade and the visions for the future.

Ifeoluwapo Adeniyi - Assistant Professor, University of Winnipeg, Canada and Author: *On the Bank of the River*

The threads of our interconnectedness with our neighbours, our environment and our universe are intriguingly presented by Francis, as he takes us on a forward-looking journey, illustrating a path out of our perceived unpredictability and chaos. Helped by valuable research, insights and anecdotes, Francis explains the '*Itakun*' or strands that interlink human DNA, quantum mechanics and even the simple pumpkin seed.

Bruce Roberts - Author: *The Godot Orange*

Francis is an idealistic realist who provides a framework, in written and diagrammatic forms. He describes how we can thrive in a state of optimism throughout life, despite its ups and downs. Quoting Einstein and Darwin, he draws upon their analogies of maintaining balance on bikes and adapting to change – which we must do. We all must learn from life's lurching yo-yo!

In this book, Francis explains our purpose is not to escape our negative experiences; but to use them to widen the scope of our experiences and blessings contained in the Journey Forward.

The 14 Principles created by the author, explore ways of achieving breakthroughs during the Journey Back when things are more challenging, and maximising advantages to achieve our highest potential when we have a greater capacity to control events in the Journey Forward. Francis' book takes us step-by step on our unique Journey.

Michael Morris - Author: *The Ones Left Behind*

BLOOMING THROUGH CHAOTIC TIMES

Your Map for Navigating Our Uncertain, Complex and Turbulent Age

Francis Niyi Akinola

Illustrations by Abbirose Adey

Publications

Blooming Through Chaotic Times

COPYRIGHT

Copyright ©Francis Niyi Akinola May 2023.

Published: May 2023 Ladey Adey Publications, Ancaster, Lincolnshire, UK

Francis Niyi Akinola has asserted his right to be identified as the author of this Work in accordance with the Copyright, Designs and Patents Act 1988.

ISBN: 978-1-913579-64-7 (Paperback).

ISBN: 978-1-913579-65-4 (E-Publication).

All rights reserved. No part of this publication may be reproduced, stored in a retrieval system, or transmitted in any form or by any means - for example, electronic, photocopy, recording - without the prior written permission of the publisher. The only exception is brief quotations in printed reviews.

British Library Cataloguing-in-Publication Data.

A catalogue record for this book is available from The British Library.

Cover Design and Illustrations by Abbirose Adey, of Ladey Adey Publications.

Neither the author nor the publisher can be held responsible for any loss, claim or damage arising out of the use, or misuse of the suggestions made, the failure to take business, financial or legal advice or for any material on third party websites.

The author assumes full responsibility for the accuracy, originality, and legality of the material contained herein.

The author and publisher have made every effort to ensure the external websites included in this book are correct and up to date at the time of going to press. The author and publisher are not responsible for the content, quality or continuing accessibility of the sites.

If you have enjoyed this book please give a review on Amazon for Francis.

DEDICATION

My Dad, Michael Araoye Akinola,
through whose Journey Back,
I'm able to sustain my Journey Forward,
and from my Journey Back
I've experienced his Journey Forward

Blooming Through Chaotic Times

CONTENTS

Dedication v
Foreword ix
Introduction 1
PART ONE: The Journey BACK 17
Chaos
    Principle 1: Life is Fragile 21
    Principle 2: Stoop to Conquer but Look Up! 41
    Principle 3: We are all Wounded 61
Coherence
    Principle 4: Consistency is Key 77
    Principle 5: Hope with Courage and Integrity 93
    Principle 6: Memory is the Vehicle out of Chaos 103
    Principle 7: Bloom Through the Path of Motherhood 119
PART TWO: The Journey Forward 137
Blooming
    Principle 8: Practice Gratitude 141
    Principle 9: Sustain Focus 157
    Principle 10: Tinker about the Edge 171
    Principle 11: Power is Service for Unity and Peace 187
Becoming
    Principle 12: Build a Legacy 207
    Principle 13: Itakun 225
    Principle 14: Parable for Living 251

Afterword: The Parable of Daddy	271
Acknowledgements	281
References	283
About The Author	291
Index	295
Notes	299

FOREWORD

You are never too old to ride the Carousel

Ladey Adey

Blooming Through Chaotic Times

Foreword

WE ALL BELIEVE in our own reality but perhaps things aren't always as they seem. Francis' book takes us through life's everyday challenges, the good, the bad and the ugly and asks us to question our 'status quo' in order to grow. Are you ready for the challenge?

Francis has a unique way of showing us the way and guiding us to make our own life affirming decisions, so you are not alone in this challenge. He has separated his message into four categories and introduced fourteen principles: seven for the Journey Back and seven for the Journey Forward. These journeys are the fabric of everyone's life and he is showing us how to circumvent the bad and ugly parts as much as possible and take the experience and develop them into the good parts!

Looking at the four categories which break down the principles and help us to take on board the new concepts.

- ◉ Chaos - a state of being which comes upon us frequently and we have to learn how to move from the journey backwards into the journey forward until we discover our new reality, balance and way of being.
- ◉ Coherence - the state which explains the discipline needed to put into practice Francis' sterling principles.
- ◉ Blooming - the state which celebrates our victories and successes making them integral values and part of our own physique as we mature.

- Becoming - the state which gives us our ultimate purpose in life, the way we conduct ourselves and give meaning to why we exist.

This is not a book for the weak-hearted but for those who want to be the best they can be.

The fourteen principles Francis has identified are clear and impactful. Whilst all are compelling and to be practiced, my favourites are Gratitude and Itakun. Gratitude is a quality to be actioned regardless of the circumstance you are presently experiencing. Itakun explores the meaning of life, unity and how we make our 'mark' in this world.

As I write this foreword, I have been transported from a successful personal and professional life, blooming and on the way to becoming, back into Chaos. Within three months I have had to deal with saying goodbye to my mother and take the painful bereavement journey and have experienced a serious health issue, a mild stroke, which has derailed my business and working capacity. Whilst I pray for the stroke effects to be temporary it brings to mind the 'yo-yo' effect which Francis explains so well in his introduction. Without the previous work outlined in the Principles and the Journey Forward, this set-back would be so much harder. In fact, it would be easy to view life from a perspective of 'victim' rather than that of 'gusto'! Overall, it is a choice!

Choices can only be taken when you are equipped with knowledge and a clear pathway of truth. This book shows Francis' passion for living a powerful life. He gives pathways to move from times of perceived weakness into new positions of strength. What is unique about Blooming Through Chaotic Times is the interweaving of paraphrase, parables and prized analogies from Francis' Yoruba culture. These stories are unfamiliar in western writing and shows how much we have to learn from the wisdom of other countries and cultures. The Alujonjonkijon fable of the Dog's Mother in the Sky is an example of this. Once read they are unforgettable and bring a new dynamic to this writing.

Francis also entwines some well documented management tools and recommends these as relevant to use for our personal life to give us more understanding.

The intriguing message contained in this book is brought to you as a continued self-awareness and development. It is not a 'how to', step by step process - it is more realistic than that! Francis sees the individual life we have as fluid, you become the person you are meant to be by flowing back and forth between the 4 states. It includes revisiting areas of life we would rather bypass. Yet, he gives Principles and tools to guide us. He acknowledges our life continues in motion and often life gets in the way of what we want to do! Unexpected turns, for instance job issues, redundancy, bereavement or a birth all have the possibility to unbalance and change our 'status quo'. How we react and respond provides choice and how we choose to use each experience to Journey Forward is important. It is a choice of this or being dragged backwards!

This is a powerful, inspirational book with numerous messages guaranteed to guide us out of chaos and into a blooming reality, one which will edify the reader and support many in bringing out the best in them. Enjoy and practise the principles so you, too, can make a difference to those you meet and interact with on a daily basis.

Ladey Adey (May 2023)

Author: Unfrozen, Successful Business Networking Online and Ara.

Blooming Through Chaotic Times

INTRODUCTION

*Without a humble but reasonable confidence
in your own powers you cannot
be successful or happy.*

Norman Vincent Peale

Introduction to the Principles

LIFE IS LIKE a yo-yo, which moves forward and backward, but this yo-yo itself has a positive momentum (moves forward). Life revolves around a point, but this revolution expands. Reality has an oscillatory and spiral momentum, and these have a forward and expansive trajectory, This trajectory of experience is what I call, 'The grand positivity of existence'.

Our experience of life comes as incidences of highs and lows, of triumphs and losses. This means throughout this book we will be looking at balancing risks during success and managing losses in the time of failures.

If we are forgetful and negligent during success, or we give up and despair during the struggle in times of failure, we can easily lose what we are labouring so hard to build.

Life has a forward trajectory, therefore we must keep moving forward, never becoming complacent with success nor letting adversity make us dejected.

Reality is Positive

Irrespective of what we go through as individuals from the forward and backward situations of life circumstances, it is important for us to bear in mind that life goes on, and attempts at retracting, diminishing, or reducing experiences for the sake of *'the good old days'* are not usually a safe bet against reality.

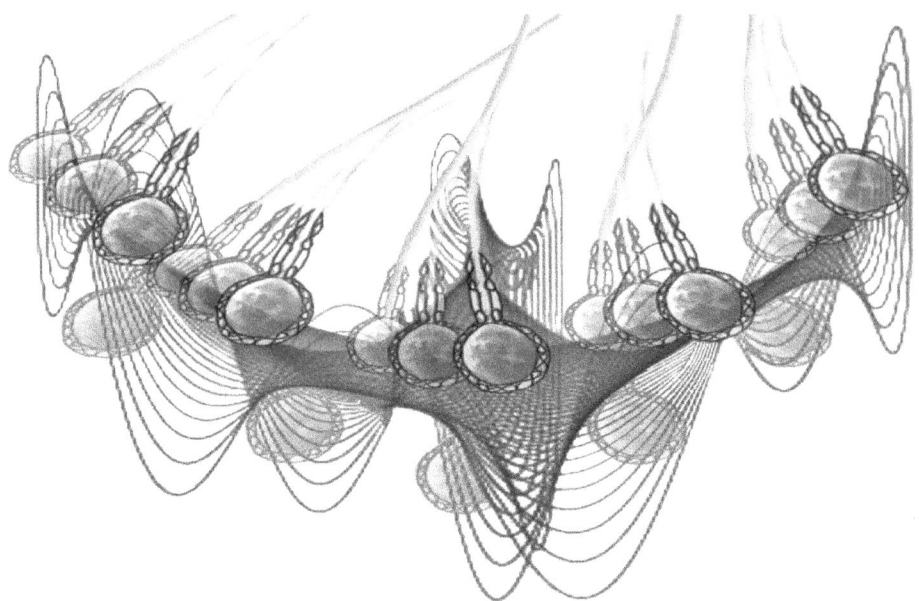

Life is like a Pendulum with a forward moving trajectory

The Big Questions

What is reality? We can say reality is an experience of existence which cannot be vanquished. The big picture of our ultimate experience will be meaningful and reasonable when it is experienced as a holistic entity, by putting all the factors surrounding our lives into play. This is what I believe the nature of reality is about.

This book explains life as ultimately positive. I describe how we can thrive and succeed through life, despite its ups and downs.

In his book, *The Strangest Secret*, Earl Nightingale gives a definition of success as, 'the progressive realization of a worthy ideal'. I use this to mean, with the right perspective we can strive to be aligned with reality ultimately as a positive continuum in life by tapping into this incremental and progressive success.

Throughout this book we shall be considering responses to important questions such as:

Introduction to the Principles

- How can we maintain an awareness of this positive perspective while embarking on the work of balancing the ups and downs of our own oscillatory experience of life?
- Why do we 'drop our guard' when we are successful?
- Why do we find it difficult to manage success?

Operating in a Positive Dimension

Operating within this forward mindset is what Norman Vincent Peale in *The Power of Positive Thinking* proposed as a 'never-ceasing flow of positive energy'. In fact, this positive outlook on life is what produces peace of mind, which is essential to improved health conditions.

By using different data and scientific research and findings, Steven Pinker also showed in his book *The Better Angels of Our Nature* how we may be living in the most peaceful times for our species' history, despite the negative vibes the media often projects. He showed how no aspect of life is untouched by the retreat from violence and how the human psyche has even grown to embrace this positive trend toward non-violence.

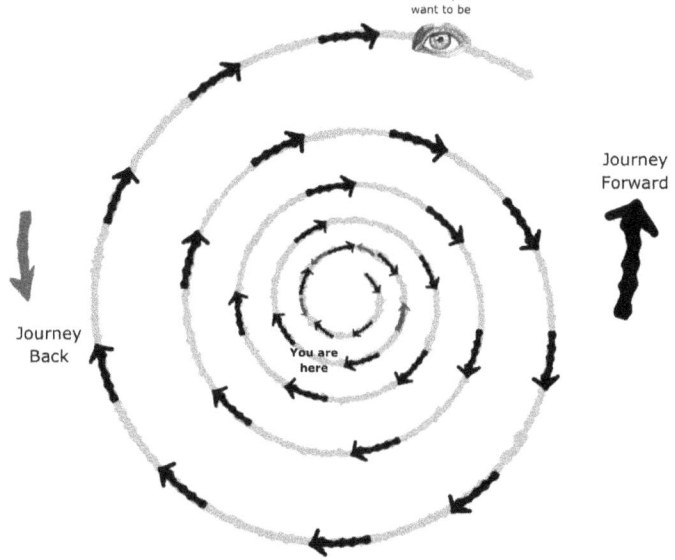

Life Spirals Back and Forth

These assertions, on a wider scale and through scientific research, have been supported by Hans Rosling in his book, *Factfulness*. In it, Rosling gives a satirical and scientific description of how ignorant we can be against global progress inequalities, poverty, violence, natural disasters, and how education, children's mortality rate and provision of modern infrastructures to better people's lives, have increased exponentially in the last 50 years.

This optimism of the universe is what we can tap into by understanding the notion of a positive and expanding reality even when life swings forward and back (yo-yos). We need to keep in mind, things get better when we develop the right mindset and attitude. By keeping abreast of the big picture, we preserve an optimism which is not just sentimental, but realistic.

The Work towards Positivity

It's not like the forward perspective of life is handed down on a platter. We have to work on it. I consider maintaining this holistic forward thrust to Albert Einstein's analogy. He said, *"Life is like riding a bicycle. To keep your balance, you must keep moving."* It is obviously awkward to ride a bicycle backward, but even riding forward it takes skill to balance. The force of propulsion keeps the movement of the bicycle going and to my mind it is the same with life.

Experiences repeat in a timeless cycle, but a good experience shrinks the struggles of the Journey Back and expands the blessings of the Journey Forward, as the following diagram suggests.

Introduction to the Principles

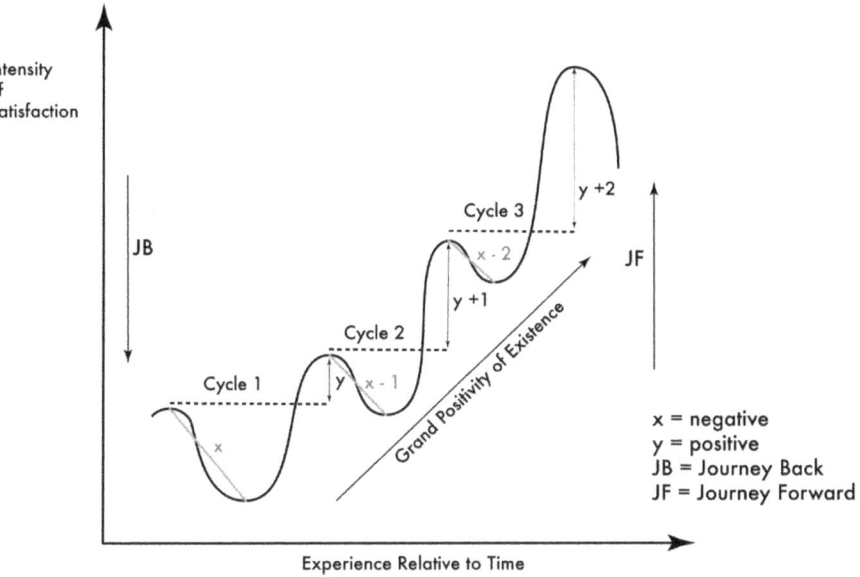

Grand Positivity of Existence

From this diagram, I aim to show how our goal is to reduce the period of Journey Back (x-1) and increase the Journey Forward (y+1) for our lives.

An ideal Journey Forward may ultimately expand to a point where the Journey Back can flow together with the Journey Forward and become a transcendental experience. This itself can agree with the positive dimension of reality.

A successful Journey Back breaks loose from a position of friction and into a Journey Forward experience of triumph, confidence, and expertise.

During the Journey Back, we mostly experience life within the control of the 'System'. By System, I mean a governing model or domain for people dealing with each other. The good news is, in the Journey Forward we break loose from the System's control and become the System ourselves.

The System, in this book, is not implied in a positive or negative perspective. The System may be a benevolent provider, mother or a heinous tyrannical father or someone inbetween. What it is for us will be dependent on our circumstances. Whichever, it is about successfully reaching our creative potential towards being our own protagonist of positivity.

Calculus and Change

It is also important to highlight how we shall experience many changes in life, and how we have to be adaptive to these changes. As the Greek philosopher, Heraclitus, said, 'The only constant is change' and as such we need to master how to put changes in perspective of our journey.

The study of Calculus, while seemingly complex, can assist us in understanding the picture of change and managing these changes in our lives.

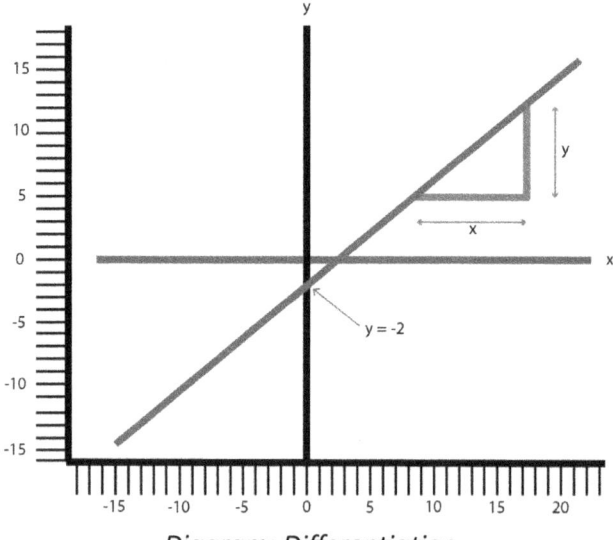

Diagram: Differentiation

This is an important model in mathematics which describes a great deal of the changes we shall be discussing. It can aid our understanding of managing change in our life.

Introduction to the Principles

Calculus calculates motion and changes in an incremental manner, and from it, we can gain an understanding of how everything changes and how in any given situation, we have to manage our life choices.

A statement attributed to Charles Darwin summarises this universal change and offers a clue to thriving through our journey, *"In the struggle for survival, it is not the strongest of the species, nor the most intelligent that survives. It is the one that is most adaptable to change."* In this book we are interested in how we adapt to life changes (struggles and blessings).

Change can be a source of stress (which is inevitable), but we have to find ways to either manage, leverage, mitigate, and accommodate this stress. By doing so, we can maximise our positive potential and maintain an integral balance of the entire process of life in a positive dimension

Mapping the Book

Blooming Through Chaotic Times presents a map for thriving in a violent, volatile, complex, unpredictable, and ambiguous age. The framework of this book is in two parts: The Journey Back and The Journeying Forward. Each of these parts, in turn, is further divided into two parts:

- ◉ Journey Back: Chaos and Coherence.
- ◉ Journey Forward: Blooming and Becoming.

The reason for making the Journey Back is either to achieve one's purpose and goals. It is for those individual stories of ours manifesting through uncomfortable experiences which require time to be articulated and resolved. When lived authentically, the Journey Back is an experience by which we attain true liberation and peace. Ideas gained from the Journey Back give us the purpose to Journey Forward.

The Journey Forward happens as a positive experience. Having thrived amidst the chaos of the Journey Back, the purpose is to keep our goals into perspective and continue to make them thrive.

This book offers Principles (14 in all) to explore ways of achieving breakthroughs during the Journey Back when things are more challenging, and maximising advantages to achieve our highest potential when we have a greater capacity to control events in the Journey Forward.

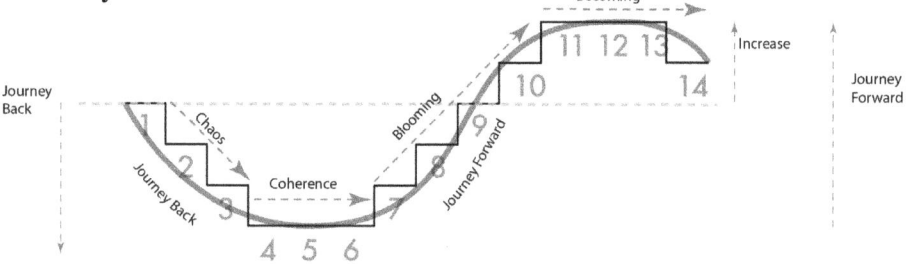

The Curvature of the Journey Back and the Journey Forward

We will consider how to widen the scope of the Journey Forward and reduce the breadth of the Journey Back through the process of error correction and emphasising positivity. Our goal is to contract our experiences during the Journey Back while expanding our experiences of our Journey Forward.

Using these two basic concepts, the Journey Back and the Journey Forward, we can develop a sustainable map to apply towards a holistic forward and expanded rhythm of life.

The 14 Principles which are depicted in the diagram at the beginning of each principle will aid readers to have a sense of the journey and to follow the progressive experience as they navigate the pages of this book.

Throughout this book, we shall learn how to approach our reality as a forward momentum amidst its expansion and

Introduction to the Principles

contraction, its pulling, bending and stretching. We will realise our 'who' and 'what' which can trump the undulating reality of our 'when' and 'where'.

Our purpose is not to escape our experiences, but to reduce the time and depth of the pain contained in the Journey Back and to widen and expand the scope of our capabilities which are contained in the Journey Forward.

This, in my opinion, is the best anyone can do to make the most from their life.

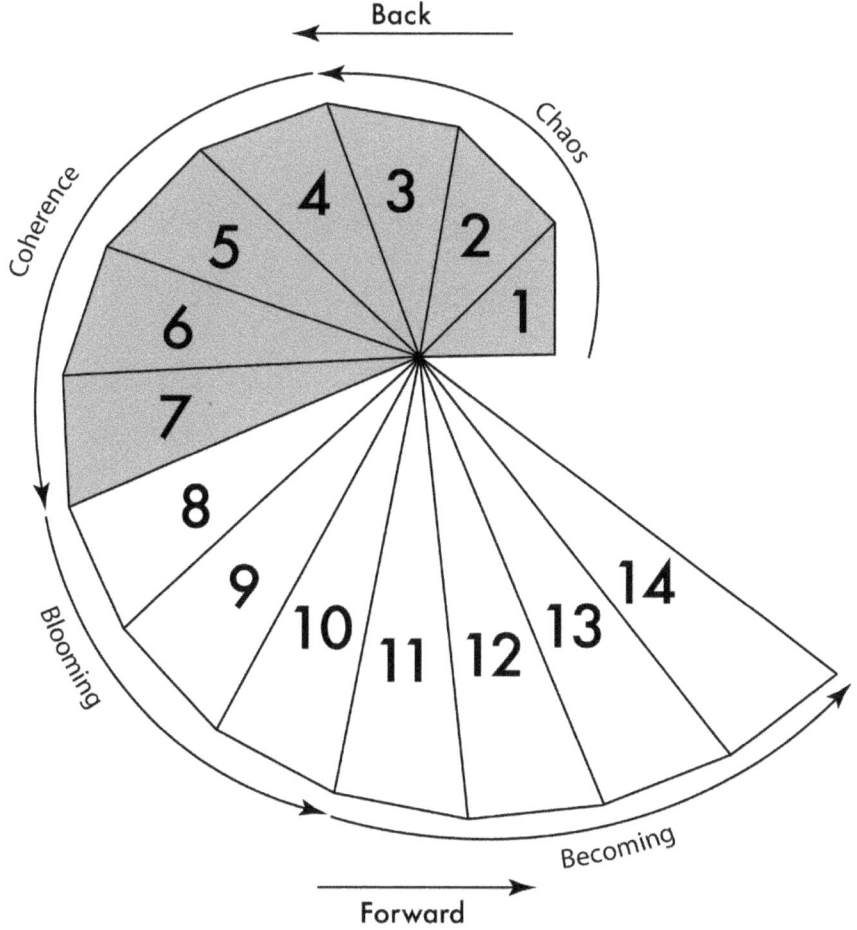

The Journey Back and Journey Forward Spiral

Some Complexities Arising from the Framework

It is impossible to divide or separate the Journey Back and the Journey Forward. They are both well integrated into our life experiences, to varying degrees, depending on our circumstances.

The book has been structured as an experiential journey in a hierarchical format. It assumes that for you to get to the next stage of experience (following principle) you must have lived and triumphed in with the presiding preceding principle. Our life's experiences do not follow a hierarchical path in real terms. It may be at best ambiguously hierarchical, but not 'mathematically' so.

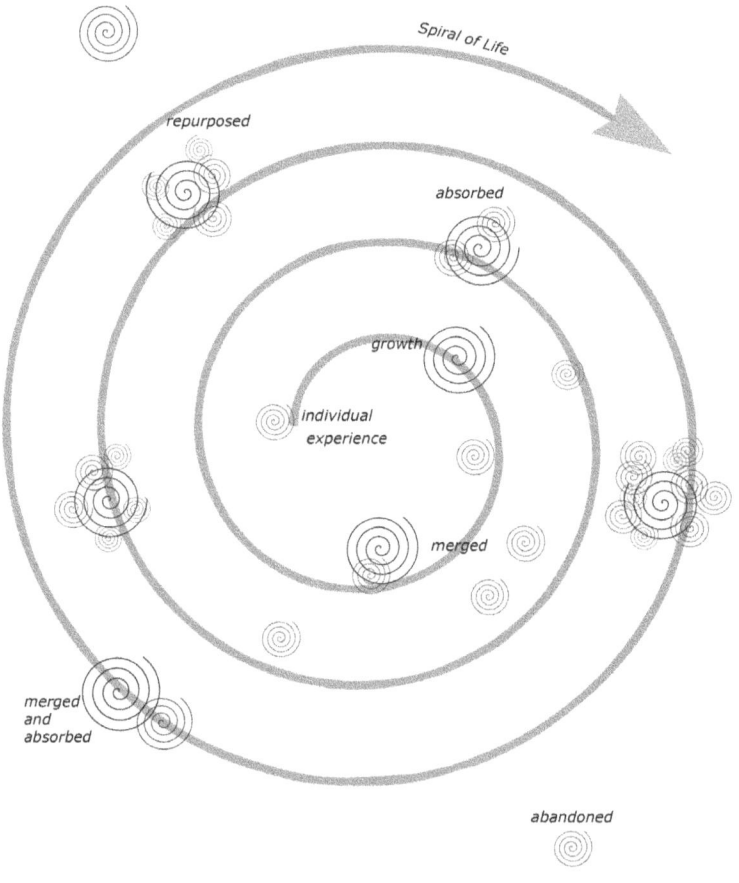

Multiplicity of Spiral Experiences

Introduction to the Principles

Multiplicity of Experiences

You may have come across Maslow's *Hierarchy of Needs*, it is a model to understand the motivation for human behaviour. For me, the 'Needs' are not necessarily hierarchical as it belittles the portrayal of the full dimension of our reality. So is the case with the Principles I will be describing.

There are a multiplicity of experiences, thus a multiplicity of Journeys which can be made towards varied purposes. To a greater or lesser degree, these purposes may merge, become absorbed by higher goals, or be abandoned unto other ideals. The important thing is to pick the most important aspects of our lives and follow these experiences.

Maslow's Hierachy of Needs

We can better appreciate the Principles of the Journey Back and Journey Forward outlined in this book by understanding how they are not sequential or proportional in the quest to maintain victory and bloom through chaotic times.

I have personally juggled the circumstances and the challenges of life, managing its ups and downs, and I have discovered they are not sequential, but simultaneous and I have discovered both the Journey Back and Forward as very integrated into a single life experience.

From the principles set forth in this book we can nurture what is being developed and is yet to bloom in our life (Journey Back), and keep safe those experiences which are already blooming (Journey Forward) within our life.

We will learn how to stay on top of policies set by the System with the correct principles; we will discover how we can live an authentic philosophy of life, and to win the war by picking the right battle.

I plan to show how to enjoy the Journey while keeping sight of the destination and to find enthusiasm, fulfilment and adventure in the Journey; not just when one arrives at the destination.

However, this is not to say these ideas are absolute and are specific to the mapped journey experience. For instance, do I have to be prepared against stress only when I go through struggles (as Principle One will show), or do I only need to be grateful when I experience a breakthrough (as the Principle Eight depicts)? This to me is a continuous life practice irrespective of the stage we are at in the journey.

All I'm saying is, these principles work, they are easy to understand and aid and enhance the progress of our life's journey. I shall share my discoveries in regard to:

1. How we can acquire the capacity to thrive and develop continually amidst every stress encountered.
2. How we can set damage controls when experiences become bad or unstable, and
3. How to apply 'sustainability' measures when experiences are good.

I shall bring out ideas and perspectives intended to enable readers, not just to better navigate through ordeals, but to thrive through them and in this thriving be able to sustain the victory of a better life.

We cannot predict life; we can only manage expectations.

Rounding Off

Blooming Through Chaotic Times is about successfully mastering life experiences while minimising its associated risks. It offers principles for lasting success which can be used by any individual, family, group, organisation or nation.

I believe by using the approach of optimism we can continually reduce and ultimately eliminate human misery and achieve human victory.

This is achieved not by cutting corners, but through an alignment with a positive reality which does not seek to deny the 'yo-yo' or spiral fabric of life, but where one can find oneself easily journeying through life much unfettered, by developing the right mentality and ability to purge the Journey Back in exchange for the illuminative Journey Forward.

In my original Yoruba culture (A culture domiciled across the globe but historically rooted in the Southwestern part of Nigeria), we say '*Atori l'aye*', which means, 'Life is a whip, which bends forward and backward'.

These positive 'yo-yo' principles can be applicable in every facet of life, and will enhance movement up the social hierarchy ladder, increasing status, wealth, and success to the extent where we become not only a problem solver but a visionary and creator.

As you work through this book you can expand on what to do and how to react on a personal level in daily circumstances of your life experience. Throughout this book, I shall play at analogies from my personal, professional, and cultural experiences. I shall apply anecdotes from Science, Management and Philosophy. The book will assist in mindset development and will encourage practical application of the thoughts shared in order to live, thrive and bloom radiantly through any chaotic crisis.

Francis Niyi Akinola (May 2023)

PART ONE
THE JOURNEY BACK

The Journey Back are those individual stories of ours manifesting through discomforting experiences which require time to be articulated and resolved.

When lived authentically, the Journey Back is an experience by which we attain true liberation and peace. Ideas gained from the Journey Back gives us the purpose to Journey Forward.

The Journey Back can manifest through personal, social or even global experiences such as the pandemic, environmental challenges (e.g global warming), or period of socio-cultural changes, hard-times which are indeed opportunities beckoning breakthrough and freedom. It is often global ordeals which filter down and can cause personal disruptions such as loss of loved ones, loss of jobs, family struggles, internal strife, mental disorders and addiction.

In fact, we experience the Journey Back through the necessities and realities of our individual lives, in our families, at our workplace, in our social lives and in every circumstance of our lives when we are faced with the frustration of discomforts and waiting.

It is important to have the right individual and collective mindset in tackling this Journey Back because they are real opportunities to bloom. Such experiences call for accountability, but they also present the chance to move forward and up in order to be free.

To refuse the responsibility to Journey Back by avoiding the work it entails would portend a far harder, longer and riskier labour with the wrong mindset. This in turn may lead us returning empty handed. Whereas those who take up the responsibility of the Journey Back, even in their weakness, often arrive at the liberating aspect of finding purpose within their individual capacities of life's journey.

Of course, this Journey Back is not an easy task. We all have an aversion to stress. Suffering takes its toll on the human psyche, and we do not know how to cope in situations of extreme discomfort. Few have any motivation to work against blatant friction and torque. However, experience points to the reality of lessons and momentum gained from such journeying back are necessary resources needed to maximise the energy for a forward conquest.

Why does the downturn weigh so much? How does it seem like there are multitudes who look at life from the perspective that they are 'losers' and nothing else can be done? Why do many people seem stuck on the losing side? Why do we give up on success? What happens when we are down and we see no freedom in sight?

The following suggested principles when practiced and applied during these periods of imposed changes will enhance our success and freedom out of chaos.

The Journey Back is positive in nature because it seeks to heal when we undertake the required work. When we refuse to implement the necessary discipline, it becomes a backward spiral, and this is where regression sets in.

Let us remember the Journey Back is not a backward journey, it has a forward trajectory.

CHAOS

The Chaos Principles (1-3)

These Principles deal with the raw circumstances of a prevailing problem and proposes the best attitude, we could take in the face of such an experience.

PRINCIPLE 1.

LIFE IS FRAGILE

Chance favours the prepared mind.

Louis Pasteur

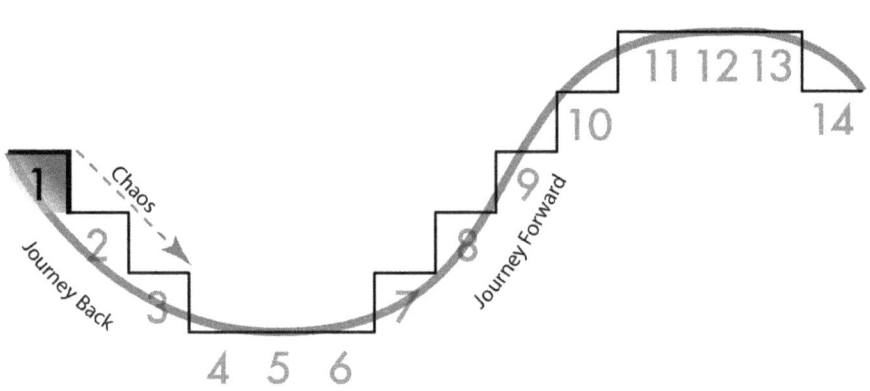

Principle 1

Principle 1: CHAOS – Life is Fragile

LET'S START FROM the reality of where you are; life can be fragile, ruthless and unfair. Everything is in a state of flux, including the status quo! We live in a violent, unpredictable, complex, and ambiguous world.

The best means of tackling the fragility of life, in my opinion, is to be proactively and purposefully prepared against its unpredictability.

By life being unpredictable, I mean that there is no absolute guarantee of anything. A student, for instance, may study, toil and burn the midnight oil but still fail in their exams. A business person may hustle and work on his business but still lose money and miss important deals. People invest so many resources into their relationship yet may still be betrayed by a partner. One may be entirely devoted to one's family and friends and still lose them, either physically or morally. All one has laboured for may be disrupted in an instant.

While the observations above may sound negative, the realisation of this fact, and setting up appropriate actions towards tackling a life anomaly would create the right foundation for the journey. Life is like the changing seasons and while we cannot change the seasons we can change ourselves.

A lesson of the Journey from British Politics

Life is filled with the unexpected. For instance, looking at the volatility in British politics, we can understand this indeterminacy of life. I would like to make some analogies.

When former British Prime Minister, David Cameron, won his second election at a landslide in 2015, he confessed that he didn't expect to win at such a margin (I am sure he did not see his exit just round the corner, either). He decided to take a massive gamble with the Brexit referendum. He succeeded in keeping Scotland in the Union, then he took a bet on Europe. Brexit caught him and almost everyone, including the winners, unaware.

Theresa May, who became Prime Minister from the aftermath of the Brexit referendum and the resignation of David Cameron in 2016, seems to have had power thrust upon her. From such lofty heights and responsibility, she took a personal gamble, the result of which in my opinion, was the beginning of her end. She called for an election in order to consolidate her 'Journey Forward' position, but the result of the election was a boomerang. She lost her authority and control at Parliament and she spiralled into a Journey Back which resulted in her ultimate loss of office.

When Boris Johnson came to power in 2019, immediately there were talks about the end of austerities measures set up as a damage control by David Cameron, because he opined that the UK has made enough savings to lift these shackles of burdens. Then out of nowhere, the Covid-19 pandemic began, followed by the 2022 Russian/Ukrainian crisis, leading to a debt-ridden economy which may be difficult to pay off for the next three generations. We cannot predict life; we can only manage expectations.

Principle 1: CHAOS – Life is Fragile

The Challenge of the Unexpected

Something may be entirely perfect today and be completely derailed tomorrow, such is life! We all woke up to the unpredictable historical events of the 2008 Financial Crisis, the election of Donald J. Trump, Brexit, Covid-19 pandemic and of Russia bombing Ukraine, events which some may argue were not very likely but which are shaping our lives today. Life is tough and fragile and we need to be prepared for eventualities, to be on our guard.

It is not our altruistic desire to survive and thrive which will make us bloom, but our realisation that man is ever so more prone to being preyed upon than to prey; it would be wise to take personal responsibility towards survival rather than assuming an overt and naïve over-dependence on any System for survival.

The System

I shall use the term 'System' throughout this book to depict a set of interconnected and interdependent social structures and institutions which put forward a set of norms and rules, procedures or policies designed to regulate and govern our lives. This includes any activity or process which regulates and maintains order and stability, particularly in politics, economics, and culture in order to achieve a common dependent goal or purpose.

How I Missed out on Instant Wealth

Here is a personal anecdote on how altruism, a naïve knowledge and dependence on the System may be detrimental.

> Some years ago, I decided to go into online Foreign Exchange Trading. I had a quick spree of training from a guy who just stumbled back from the financial crash of 2008.

I thought I was ready and my initial investment of £2000 generated a return of over £10,000 while I was sleeping.

This was soon after I started trading, so my assumption of online trading was 'Life is a bed of roses for traders'. After years of toils and hardships of trying to make ends meet, I thought, I had hit my 'golden enterprise' at last! I was about to find out - life is indeed fragile.

Within a month of my trading, my investment rose to £10,000. I kept looking, doing nothing, watching the 'free' money rise and rise. I did not know the art of risk management, I had no plans for 'stop-loss', no limits, no hedging or diversification. I did not realise trading in the Foreign Exchange is like life - it is a Yo-Yo!

One day, asleep, I dreamt of the rise and rise of my investment to over £200,000. On waking up and full of expectations, I got up and went straight to my computer, I saw red. The entire money was gone and I was in deficit!

From a massive green of over £10,000, within a night, I spiralled down from a prince to a pauper. My email was filled with warnings from the online trading provider about the risk of going bankrupt on the platform if I did not top up my fund. I panicked. I immediately went to my bank, withdrew £1,000 and deposited this on the platform, hoping, at least to recoup my initial investment, but instead, the fall continued down and down and down.

What the Experienced Know

I remember how during those days I was scrambling all over for assistance on how I would be rescued from my loss. I was in conversation with my financial consultant on

Principle 1: CHAOS – Life is Fragile

the trading platform and he said, *"Can't you see the money is lost?"* and advised me to sell off.

But I held on because I was too horrified to let go, but this not letting go led me deeper and deeper down the rabbit hole of loss.

Rather than admitting my fate, I continued to pump the little savings I had into the platform, I went into my bank overdraft, then I used my credit card. I did not come to my senses until I was bankrupt, both on the online platform and my bank.

There is a saying, *'If you haven't passed through an ordeal and claim you are wise, who then is your teacher?'* This time was a very difficult period. My ego would not allow me to accept any damage or damage control. I suddenly began to realise what I was: a gambler, not an investor.

Luck without Discipline

Every investor is a gambler but not every gambler is an investor. The difference can be shown in the level of discipline. I am naturally an open person and a risk taker but I realised life is more than passion and excitement, it is also about putting a risk mitigation system in place to prevent or limit any loss.

> A few years later, I was working in one of the London casinos, I witnessed a young man who played a £20 game and won over £30,000. He was lauded and his pictures littered the floor of the gambling shop as the company made to boost the profile of his wins in order to attract more players.
>
> He came back to the casino the following week and squandered all the money he had won. Like his fortune, his loss also became well known. He resulted to violence,

started breaking the casino's louvered screens and drinking glasses. The police were called and he was arrested.

Don't Bet on Positivity Without Preparation

These are the sort of stories many of us have lived through, to a larger or lesser degree, and at one time or another, from which we have learned lessons we all can share. It is often said in trading and gambling, "You cannot beat the floor." The 'floor' here is the trading platform set up to enable the betting process. But on a larger scale, the floor depicts a System, out of which life's process runs, and which will seek to profit out of any individual naivety and carelessness.

The System is Not Unfair

The System's motive is to align the domain with its own objectives. This may not be entirely aligned with our personal purpose.

The process by which we fulfil our motives (in spite of our present circumstances) requires careful planning, because the odds forcing our conformance with the System far outweigh our internal and external resources to breakthrough.

It is important we do not conclude the System is being malicious, even when its working objective may currently not be in line with our purpose. The System has actually attended to our survival and we have thus far stayed alive because of our social contract with the System to keep it sustained.

We can see everywhere this overt reliance on the System, whether the System be corporations, state or nation. It expects our reliance without factoring in our personal responsibility towards self-actualisation.

Remember this, if the System is torn between its own survival and ours, it would preserve itself at the detriment of ours. It is one thing to realise the intent of the System, it is another to work at putting our own fate and survival into our own hands by learning how to bloom through the potential chaos of the System!

Our Task Within the System

Although you could be a cog within the System, you may find yourself living a life which ultimately is not of your choosing. Your purpose is to thrive and bloom, to live a life which ultimately is one which you are meant for.

It is necessary to appreciate the benefits of the System, for, without law and order, checks and balances introduced by the System – albeit, possibly curbing your potential, we will individually be more susceptible to a mutual destruction of one another.

In order to build momentum and thrive within the System, we have to be proactive and purposefully prepared. We need to begin by setting goals. Purpose begins with goals. Here is a list of goals you could choose (note these are not SMART goals):

- ◉ Earn a degree.
- ◉ Get a job.
- ◉ Obtain a promotion.
- ◉ Achieve a certain level of income.
- ◉ Learn a new skill or subject.
- ◉ Lose weight.
- ◉ Improve physical and mental strength and endurance.
- ◉ Quit smoking or alcohol.
- ◉ Pay off debt.
- ◉ Invest in stocks.
- ◉ Start a business.

- ◎ Learn a new language.
- ◎ Improve social skills.
- ◎ Make new friends.
- ◎ Get married.
- ◎ Start a family.
- ◎ Write a book.
- ◎ Compose music.
- ◎ Reduce carbon footprint.
- ◎ Improve productivity.
- ◎ Develop a greater sense of purpose and meaning.

The Obligation to Prepare and Plan

Rather than betting against the fragility of existence by a misconstrued assumption of an easy-go-get-lucky safety based on a false reliance of the System, it is safer and more reasonable to take responsibility to safeguard oneself against life's changes. The best preparation is putting hope into the action of planning whilst preparing against the worst.

Planning is the foundation of what is taught in every management programme. Luck meets a prepared and proactive mind: a mind

S   Specific
M Measurable
A Achievable
R Relevant
T Time-bound

which does not procrastinate but makes hay while the sun shines by seizing every opportunity to do what is worthwhile while he still can.

A combination and reflective use of SWOT and PESTEL analysis have enabled us to continually manage our enterprise at ARC and You, Framat, and ARC Facilities. By using a continual feedback loop from customers, we are better able to improve on services and to better navigate the complexities of global and local occurrences such as Covid-19, Brexit and cost of living crisis and to develop a more engaging and streamlined process.

We may see the notion of planning and preparation as very basic tenets which should be realised and acted upon by everyone. In spite of this common knowledge, its application is quite uncommon because of the personal responsibility which is involved.

I shall describe some common analytical steps, which I have employed in my own personal activities and have proved useful towards achieving success. These are taught in management school and courses but if applied in everyday life it would aid everyone to be better prepared against chaos.

Make your Goals SMART

While we have identified our goals, it is important to break the process down in chunks to enable its implementation in a non-overwhelming manner.

SMART goals were developed by George Doran, Arthur Miller and James Cunningham they have been adopted in management. The term, SMART is an acronym that stands for Specific, Measurable, Achievable, Relevant, and Time-bound. Here is a breakdown of each component:

Specific: Goals should be well-defined and clear. They should answer the *'what,' 'why,'* and *'how'* of what you want to achieve. For example, *"I want to lose 10 pounds in the next three months by exercising and eating a healthier diet."*

Measurable: Goals should be quantifiable, so that progress can be tracked and measured. For example, *"I will track my weight loss progress every week and aim to lose 2-3 pounds per week."*

Achievable: Goals should be challenging but attainable. It's important to set goals that are realistic and within your capabilities. For example, if you've never exercised before, setting a goal to run a marathon in three months is likely to be unachievable.

Relevant: Goals should be relevant to your overall objectives and aligned with your values. For example, if your overall objective is to live a healthier lifestyle, setting a weight loss goal is relevant.

Time-bound: Goals should have a specific deadline for completion. This helps to create a sense of urgency and helps to track progress. For example, *"I will achieve my weight loss goal of 10 pounds in the next three months."*

P	Political
E	Economical
S	Social
T	Technological
E	Environmental
L	Legal

Principle 1: CHAOS – Life is Fragile

Watch out for the Hawks

Chaos usually happens when we let down our guard against risk. A simple way of determining what sort of personal or organizational risk to guard against is to analyse where the risk comes from. Francis Aguilar, a professor in strategic planning, used the acronym of PESTEL as a method where we can identify and prepare against external risks.

The acronym PESTEL stands for Political, Economic, Sociocultural, Technological, Environmental, and Legal. We can use it to reduce risk while working through the ordeals of life.

Here's a brief explanation of each factor:

Political: This refers to government policies and regulations.

Economic: This factor looks at the overall economic conditions and trends such as inflation, interest rates, exchange rates and economic growth.

Sociocultural: This factor considers the social and cultural factors including lifestyle trends which may create dysfunction.

Technological: This factor examines the technological advancements that could impact a day to day living.

Environmental: This factor considers how the natural environment can impact our lifestyle and includes factors such as climate change and natural disasters.

Legal: This factor examines the laws and regulations which impact our lives, such as health and safety regulations, labour laws, etc.

By analysing each of these factors, we can gain a better understanding of the external environment and make informed decisions about our lives.

Guard Against the Internal Enemy

Using these tools helps us to understand where we are in our Journey Back. But we also have an internal enemy which is ourselves. So, another useful tool, accredited to a number of business gurus in the 1960s, called SWOT analysis, could assist self-reflection and awareness and enable us to better prepare against the tides of time.

The acronym SWOT stands for Strengths, Weaknesses, Opportunities, and Threats. This acronym is used in problem solving and decision making and works towards mapping out the best and most practicable path of survival and thriving.

Here is a brief explanation of each component:

Strengths: This refers to the internal factors that give individuals, communities or organisations an advantage, a potential which can be further explored. These can include reputation, proprietary technology, talent, strong financial position and uniqueness.

Weaknesses: This looks at the internal factors which put an individual, community or organisation at a disadvantage. These can be a lack of certain educational qualifications or a lack of confidence in certain respects.

Opportunities: This factor looks at the external factors that could create new opportunities for individuals, communities and organizations. These can include things like changes in government policies, emerging grants, or new technological know-how.

Threats: This looks at the external factors which could negatively impact individuals, communities or organisations. These can include things like changes in government regulations, increased economic downturns or natural disasters.

Principle 1: CHAOS – Life is Fragile

S   Strength
W   Weakness
O   Opportunities
T   Threats

Applying SMART, PESTEL and SWOT to Manage Risk

By a combination of these techniques, we can gain a better understanding of our external and internal environment and develop a more effective plan to better prevent chaos from happening to us through gradual implementation of these techniques in risk control processes.

In the likelihood of a threat, one can be better prepared to manage risks by setting out plans to either **Avoid, Reduce, Transfer, Share** or **Accept the Risks**.

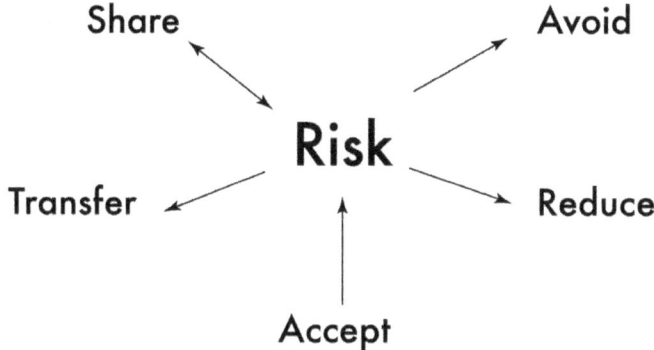

Such undertakings are the basis of modern Systems within organisations and we can also apply these in our individual lives. For instance, we buy insurance to guard against risks. Risks such as, being hit by an uninsured driver; from theft or damage in our house. What other risks do we need to consider when planning our fragile life?

The Risk Nature and Man Can Pose

Chaos out of the fragility of life may also come from either nature or man, or a combination of both. In spite of existing in an age of rapid evolution and progress, it would be a mistake to assume that the current state of progress has eliminated the negative impact of evolution and that of a 'survival of the fittest'.

Things are good because good people work at creating Systems which are beneficial to humanity and this should not be taken for granted. Recent political, environmental and economic issues in the world have shown how fragile the assumption of goodness may be if there is not enough commitment from all of us to sustain its efficacy.

When the work of equality and fairness is ignored and not proactively worked at, many will descend into their base animal nature of bitterness, anger, envy and resentment.

A good example of how nature and man can cause descent into chaos out of an evolutionary case of 'survival of the fittest' can be related to the effect of global warming in Nigeria between the arable farming south and the herding and grazing north side of Nigeria.

The Nigerian Herdsman and the Farmer

A simple herdsman from the north and a simple farmer from the south may be out of consonance with the origin of how the calamity befalling them originated from the 'industrial revolution' from a far-off land called the United Kingdom.

Rearing cattle is not simply an economic action for a Fulani herdsman in Northern Nigeria, it is a legacy bestowed by his ancestors. He must continue the legacy by rearing cattle and providing for them through grazing, but he has come to realise that things have changed. The once lush grassland in the north for rearing his cattle freely is no

Principle 1: CHAOS – Life is Fragile

more available (as a result of global warming) and he has to force his way south to continue the legacy by providing for his cattle, which to him is an obligation.

On an equal note, the simple farmer of the south has his land bequeathed by his ancestral family both as a means of subsistence and as a legacy. He has an obligation to use this land as a means of preservation of his family and ancestry. Now, he has the desperate Fulani herdsman encroaching his land. Anyone can imagine the consequence, and this is one of the reasons for the insecurity in Nigeria.

These two men who are completely oblivious that the root of their crisis of survival is caused by the economic motive of people living 6,000 miles away.

Without a continual careful analysis and methodical planning and development of what works, issues (such as those described in the Nigerian farming story) which are not usually caused by us, can cause us to easily spiral into chaos.

Be Prepared

Psychologists have argued, 'The only reality is pain.' Any chaos introduces pain, and we are often faced with the frustration of waiting, which is worsened when the waiting period is undefined. We become victims and life becomes an endless horizon of waiting for time and chance to happen. This is tough.

What is your 'Plan B'? We not only need to think about this, but we also have to articulate it and start working on the plan. This is relevant both for the Journey Back and the Journey Forward. A 'Plan B' is even more essential for the Journey Back because here we are more fragile, evolution is more ruthless in this state and can easily take an ungrounded, unprepared person down.

When life beats you down and you are at a point of loss, take courage, look beyond the horizon, and re-imagine, believe it is all going to make sense soon. This experiential condemnation will be a commencement of freedom. So, by being purposefully and proactively prepared, we can create gain from crisis. This will fulfil the truism of philosopher Friedrich Nietzsche's words, "What does not kill you will make you stronger'.

Change and decay are the constants of this life, and as such it is best to have an attitude of planning.

Preparedness Is Not An Absolute Guarantee

Plan B can be considered a worthwhile strategy. It allows chance to favour the prepared mind, to make hay while the sun shines, or even to dig our well before we are thirsty, but it is not an absolute guarantee of escaping chaos. The plethora of factors needed to mitigate against calamity makes it next to impossible to plan for almost every eventuality. Sometimes, the issue may not be action, the issue may lie in the determination of what is worth actioning.

The accomplishment of our purpose in spite of our astuteness and preparedness is not even foolproof from chaos which may still beat us down. Change and decay are the constants of this life, and as such it is best to have an attitude of planning.

So, we may ask, what can we do within this seeming chaos? The best we can do is to be proactive at planning. We must continually plan, even when there is no guarantee of the plan coming to fruition.

Murphy's Law

This reminds me of *Murphy's Law*. Murphy's law is a popular adage which states, '*Anything that can go wrong, will go wrong*'. It reflects a broader truth: that no matter how carefully we plan, unexpected events and challenges are an inevitable part of life.

As such, the best approach is often to prepare as thoroughly as possible, remain flexible and adaptable, and keep a sense of humour when things go wrong.

Planning and preparation against the calamities of existence, even when there is no absolute guarantee of the plan working, is the most we can do at confronting the fragility of existence. These two actions are our greatest chance for freedom which trumps the chaos which will arise at some point in our life.

Mike Tyson once said, *"Everybody has a plan until you get punched in the face."* If thriving is not a guarantee for one who plans, we can only imagine what happens when one does not.

The Consequences of Not Planning

Plans may not suffice since life still deals blows from the most unexpected source. How much worse would it be then for someone who does not and has not cultivated an attitude of planning and who treats life's experiences with unplanned levity?

If we do not develop an adequate System of planning and preparation for life's unexpected circumstances then we are so much more at risk to chaos.

What if We are Already in Chaos?

We must want to thrive and set stock on achieving success by preventing chaos in our lives. Even if we are already in chaos we must want to know how we can survive in spite of it, or get out of it completely.

Nothing is too chaotic that it cannot produce useful valuable buds and thus bloom. Our life's task is to work out of the disorder, to accept it and move through it and convert it into order and meaningfulness. Denying chaos or betting on its evolutionary survival (the end result justifying the means) can lead to ever-deeper chaos. Principle 2: Stoop to Conquer but Look Up describes the attitude we must assume in order to get out of chaos.

Practical suggestions for confronting the Fragility of Life

1. Make a list of what you would like to achieve (goals).
2. Write down a self-reflection analysis of your strengths and weaknesses.
3. What are the current PESTEL challenges which may affect your goals?
4. Using the SMART model write simple steps to achieve your goals.

PRINCIPLE 2.
CHAOS
STOOP TO CONQUER BUT LOOK UP!

The way up is down.

Søren Kierkegaard

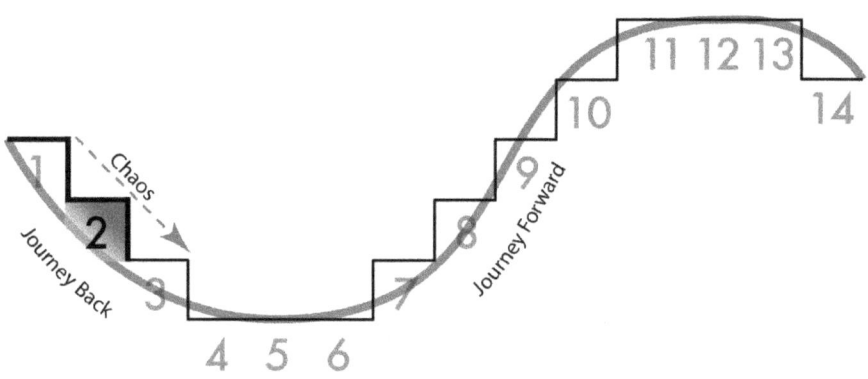

Principle 2

Principle 2: CHAOS – Stoop To Conquer But Look Up

To live well we must find our way up out of the chaos? The way up from this pit is down! We must stoop to conquer. Stooping to conquer means adopting a role, position, attitude, behaviour or undertaking, which is often seen as being beneath one's abilities or social position in order to achieve one's end.

Stooping Within the Prevailing Culture

We are living within a culture of ostentatiousness, extravagance, and self-expression. Cultural phenomena such as social media platforms have enabled people to curate and broadcast their lives to a wider audience than ever before. This increases the pressure to present oneself in an eye-catching and attention-grabbing way, giving rise to a boom of influencers and content creators, many of whom are known for their flamboyant personalities and lifestyles.

In such an age of power and drive for prominence and stardom, to bide one's time in lowliness is not always perceived as a cool objective and may be seen as antithetical to the popular culture of entitlement and the 'must have NOW' attitude.

A mindset towards waiting foretells our capacity for future and lifelong success. This is well demonstrated in the popular

Marshmallow Experiment of Delayed Gratification conducted by psychologist, Walter Mischel. This simple psychological experiment is where marshmallows are placed in front of pre-school children. The children are given the option of either waiting until the coordinator returns, in order to get a bigger treat, or if they would rather not wait, to settle for a less-desired treat.

The children were put into a room and secretly observed. The coordinator measured the time it would take for a child to wait before succumbing to munching the treat. In this manner, he could measure their resolve to see if they have the ability to wait and delay their gratification.

Research has shown that the children who were willing to delay gratification and have waited until the coordinator returns, ended up having higher SAT scores, lower levels of substance abuse, lower likelihood of obesity, better responses to stress, stronger social skills as reported by their parents, and generally higher scores in a range of abilities.

This shows how integral patience is to success. Demanding instant gratification ultimately encourages ruin.

Why Wait?

Waiting is not easy, but it is with this patience one builds the strength to thrive. There is so much to learn and to master that we must develop the work which allows expertise to take root before coming out as established. After we must have highlighted a worthwhile cause to pursue, it is wise to wait for it to grow and bloom.

The ability of being contented in seeming obscurity until one develops enough capability for a persistent blooming depends on whether one has found a solid purpose which is worth the wait.

If the children in the Marshmallows experiment did not have the promise of a larger treat, obedience may still test their resolve, but motivation may not be truly satisfied. For a worthy wait an adequate motive must be clearly defined.

Why Stoop?

It is by stooping we build the foundation of our future blooming and become more content and happy in life. The taller and stronger the edifice we wish to build, the deeper and entrenched the foundation must be.

To stoop down is necessary, but it is worthless if we are content with the downward view. We must look up. Looking up means believing in a purpose larger than ourselves. By waiting and honing our desire, we can conquer whatever barrier hinders us in reaching our goals.

The only way to do great work is to love what you do. If you haven't found this love yet, keep looking. If you have discovered what you would like to achieve or attain, do not hurry to showcase your attainment, stoop, build your foundation and allow it to mature.

We all obviously need inspiration and mentors to guide our journey to freedom, but ultimately, we have a responsibility to discover our uniqueness and to work at fulfilling our life goals. From now on, I will use the term purpose rather than goal because a purpose will make us journey farther.

The Difference Between Purpose and Goals

Purpose and goals are related concepts, but they have different meanings and implications.

Purpose refers to an underlying reason or motivation for doing something. It is the larger, overarching reason for existence or for pursuing a particular course of action. Purpose answers the question of 'why' something is being done. It provides the context for goals and helps to guide decision-making and behaviour.

Goals, on the other hand, refer to specific, measurable objectives which are intended to be achieved within a certain time frame and bring about a desired result. They answer the question of 'what' is to be achieved.

Examples to demonstrate this difference could be: the purpose of a business might be to provide innovative solutions to meet customers' needs, while a specific goal might be to increase revenue by 10% in the next quarter. Or, in a domestic scenario, the purpose is to live a healthier life and a specific goal to lose 6lbs in 4 weeks. Fulfilling a purpose may entail setting up a series of goals.

Why Do We Need To Look Up?

Purpose is about having meaning, developing reason, your 'why' which is superior to your chaos and makes the struggle worthwhile.

Where does purpose come from? It comes from being true to our experiences. It comes from living our realities intensely. It comes from discovering our uniqueness which makes us 'stand out from the crowd'.

No two human beings are exactly the same, not even identical twins. However, despite the immediate dangers of standing out it is far more dangerous to remain simply as a conformist, at the base of the hierarchy, where the stoop is enforced. It is only when a purpose is resilient, brave and unique enough that a journey generates momentum and gains speed on conquering the path to freedom.

Standing out takes courage, we often avoid standing out too much as it is difficult and can induce ridicule, despite this it should not be ignored. It is from our uniqueness we understand our why, and if our why is deep enough, we can develop the capacity to bear its struggles.

A Beautiful Admonishment About Your Uniqueness

Strong admonishment and advice was given by Steve Jobs in his famous commencement speech to Stanford University graduates in 2005. He made it clear how we need to look up and use our uniqueness to thrive. He said,

> *"You've got to find what you love. And that is as true for your work as it is for your lovers. Your time is limited, so don't waste it living someone else's life.*
>
> *Don't be trapped by dogma — which is living with the results of other people's thinking. Don't let the noise of other's opinions drown out your own inner voice.*
>
> *And most important, have the courage to follow your heart and intuition. They somehow already know what you truly want to become. Everything else is secondary."*

It is your duty to discover your uniqueness and explore your potential. Uniqueness can be very diverse. It may be about talents and skills, personality traits, life experiences, physical characteristics or interests and a combination of them all.

What Stooping is Not

Stooping is not about wallowing about in an inferiority complex (or similar) but about beginning humbly with a fulfilling actualisation in mind. By stooping, we accept the tentative irrelevance of our state in the eyes of others, while working on matters close to our heart with a sense of our own worth, uniqueness, and purpose.

There are many who are downcast, not because of their state, but because their mind convinces them they are worthless and of little use. In this mindset, they risk their entire system collapsing before they even try to look up. They may survive but not thrive. I am aware, one of the most difficult works we have to do is that of building confidence, but the forlornness, lack of motivation, and despair about our state is what we have to work against.

Any malicious System aims first not at your money or your life, but at rooting out confidence about yourself. This is further soured if you buy into resentment, malice and anger at what the System has made of you.

Humility and subtlety are tools needed to pass through the coercive forces of those who do not understand us and insist on blocking our purpose by using conformity.

I have seen this lack in confidence in people who have been forced into complete conformance and are dominated by the System. So much so, they have become the victim of an ideology of lack of self-belief, apathy, lack of motivation and complete acceptance of their downtrodden state.

What Do We Do While Stooping?

We need to begin by creating and developing lifelong skills toward a long-lasting adventure. This period of our obscurity should be used in preparation to achieve our purpose, not a time which draws us into resentment, anger, or arrogance.

Stooping is where we nurture our potential for blooming and develop our purpose and vision with a careful plan and strategy,

Do not waste valuable time chatting endlessly about the politics of any domain you find yourself in, instead use these times in focusing and working on yourself. We have various examples of time-wasting all around us: for instance, while relaxation is necessary, how much time do we spend drinking, clubbing, gaming, and in political and social chats? Spend your 'obscure' years developing skills and being educated. To bloom through chaotic times, we need to withdraw from harmful and wasteful activities, and strive to develop strategies and skills for building viable work and valuable networks.

The period of stooping is a time to, *'Stay hungry and stay foolish'* as stated by Steve Jobs, meaning be curious to learn and dare to be unconventional. The American businessman, Ray Davis, also said *"Patience is not passive waiting. Patience is active acceptance of the process required to attain one's goals and dreams."*

Confronting Wrongs

If we are to lead with a strong purpose and vision, we must first master the art of follower-ship and bide our time, but this should not be to the detriment of confidence.

If we cannot follow rules correctly, we will break them incorrectly, and to our ruin. So many rules are waiting to be broken if we are to grow and liberate ourselves and others. For instance, standing up for what is right by engaging in legal protest against unjust policies or laws is a courageous act requiring an underlying strong purpose by those, who first are able to abide by rules, not by those who are only disgruntled and frustrated with life.

Also, you may need to take a moral stance and report unethical behaviours by being a whistle-blower. In theses cases, you must first be sure you are not one culpable of a similar offence, thus avoiding the maxim, 'Those who live in glass houses should not throw stones.'

Ultimately, an authentic and lasting elimination of tyranny and repression requires a disciplined mindset with a passion for justice, else it's all for nothing!

The Required Work Toward Breakthrough

To ensure we do not lose confidence, we must devote ourselves to education. By engagement and careful devotion to learning, we can educate ourselves towards freedom! As mentioned earlier, we ought not to be in a hurry to be noticed early. Stay down to learn and be educated to master the art of thriving. Respect, humility and focus on study will free us from any repression which seems to press us downward. *Bide your time!*

Two interesting stories which narrate the process of patient waiting and working in obscurity in order to progress are from the movies, *The Shawshank Redemption* and *Prison Break*.

These two stories describe the great benefits of stooping in order to conquer. They depict this attitude of patiently waiting. Ironically, both narratives feature escape from prison and how any determined, forward-looking person can use the principle of stooping towards a route out of an impossible circumstance.

The Shawshank Redemption

The Shawshank Redemption is a 1994 American drama film.

The film follows the story of Andy Dufresne, a successful banker sentenced to life in prison for the murder of his wife and her lover, a crime he did not commit.

As the years pass, Andy uses his banking expertise to help the prison staff with their finances and becomes an invaluable asset to the corrupt warden, Norton. Andy eventually gains Norton's trust and is allowed to create a library for the inmates, which helps him gain even more respect from the prisoners. Along the way, he also exposes corruption of the prison staff.

However, despite his seemingly content life in prison, Andy is determined to prove his innocence and escape. While in prison he clandestinely engineered an escape by digging a hole in his prison cell. The tunnel he excavated led him to a space between two walls of the prison where he found a sewer main line.

Over the course of many years, he develops an elaborate plan to tunnel out of his cell and escape to Mexico. He painstakingly and steadfastly spent years digging the wall, revealing a tunnel just wide enough for a man to crawl into at night.

In the end, Andy's plan succeeds, he escapes from prison, leaving behind evidence which exposes Norton's corruption and the truth about his wrongful conviction.

The movie is widely regarded as a classic and has been praised for its powerful performances, stunning cinematography, and its portrayal of the triumph of hope and friendship over adversity.

Prison Break

Prison Break is a television drama series that aired on Fox from 2005 to 2009 and later returned for a fifth season in 2017.

The series follows the story of Michael Scofield, a structural engineer who deliberately got himself sent to the same prison as his brother Lincoln because he was convinced of Lincoln's innocence.

Michael orchestrates a plan to break both of them out of prison. He formulates a grand escape plan to break both of them out from prison. Michael's elaborate plan involves tattooing the prison's layout on his body, manipulating the prison's infrastructure, and building various tools and gadgets to aid in their escape.

Over the course of the series, Michael and Lincoln face numerous obstacles and challenges as they try to escape and clear Lincoln's name. They must navigate the politics and rivalries within the prison, evade the authorities who are trying to capture them, and outwit the powerful organization that has framed Lincoln.

The series has been praised for its thrilling plot, strong performances, and intricate storytelling. It has won numerous awards.

Between Breakout and Redemption

I refer to these dramas as it is worth noting how the main characters have wisely used a situation of lowliness to patiently outwit the system to the discovery of a route of escape from injustice, tyranny, and slavery. The characters apply a carefully crafted plan through the analysis of every risk involved to bloom out from their chaos.

Despite our lowly and humble state, we need to constantly look up and have a readied destination in view and refuse to cultivate an 'impossible' mindset as Andy and Michael had. This is where many people get it wrong. They fall prey to the cruelty of their circumstances and despair of their state.

Freedom requires hopeful and careful tending, and as Martin Luther King Jr. would opine, the long moral universe may eventually bend toward justice, but simply waiting without action breeds impossibility to the cause.

Waiting humbly can feel like a long hazardous road, but when we work while we wait, when we learn through the humble path of following, when we are obedient and refuse to be arrogant, when we focus on the destination while working devotedly on the journey, we break through ancient barriers and open wide the door of freedom and liberation!

Paying Attention to the Underdog

Confidence building can be a lifetime work. It might feel Herculean in proportion to the extent to which a person or an entire culture has been terribly battered into subservience by a System.

Colonialism and slavery were once such Systems which brought many black people into a forced stoop and an eradication of confidence. There has been a historical battering of many black minds into a 'Colonial mentality' (Kolomental, as Fela Anikulapo Kuti would define it) at the very best, and a slave mentality, in its worst form.

I have often observed such subservience in many. People would argue about the impossibility of fulfilling one's potential or finding one's voice, as a Black person.

Often, I wonder what the fate of the downtrodden would be if there was no such cry and bullishness of the mainstream media against such injustices, yet there are still numerous suffering in the world to be highlighted.

In my opinion, I see institutional prejudices are not so much a problem of the law as it is an issue of a lack of authentic education and experience.

Martin Luther King Jr. once also said: *"It may be true that the law cannot change the heart, but it can restrain the heartless."* While laws are made in certain countries to address such anomalies, reality shows restraining hearts do not change them. A true educational engagement is thus required to ensure a fair, equal society.

The Need to Keep Faith

Losing faith creates a loser mentality. Drawing a lesson from a Chess board game, we see how it may be difficult for a pawn to move to the other side of the board in a Chess game, but it is not impossible. When the pawn succeeds at reaching the other side of the board, it possesses a freedom that not even the king of the board has, it has the option to turn itself into whoever it wishes, therefore the pawn must keep faith.

Experiential struggles cannot be won by force but by developing a firm and tactical method of escape through a commitment to knowledge.

You fight to win, or at least to retreat in order to fight another day, not in order to lose and damn the consequences for everyone.

For instance, the many occurrences of gun violence and wars are a pathological show of despair unto nihilism. When you use brute force, rather than exercising intelligence and restraint to gain something, you are most likely already fighting a lost cause.

Breakthroughs happen through lifelong learning and careful practice. From these processes, we can create spaces for long-term actions whose results have the potential of compounding when we (like the pawn) keep the faith.

Contrary to the language of modern culture, there are vast opportunities to be found in years of obscurity when one works in the dark for an ideal which one believes in. This intense desire to realise a purpose in spite of the misunderstanding of the System becomes greatly beneficial.

The hidden years of persistently developing a passion are what creates the potential towards confidence which enables us to break through to clarity, understanding and freedom.

Principle 2: CHAOS – Stoop To Conquer But Look Up

The System cannot see this, but the System itself is waiting for you to grow out of this obscurity in order to rescue it from the chaos and from the mouth of the dungeon in which it is condemned, as illustrated in the allegory of *Where Freedom Lies*.

Where Freedom Lies

Once, in the land of Duniyan, Chaos was the order of the day. The 401 gods who guarded the nine ancient gates of Duniyan were incapacitated by Chaos who reigned supreme, plundering the people of the land.

No one was capable of stopping this carnage and everyone was intimidated by Chaos, gods and men alike. There was an urgent necessity to escape from this carnage which exasperated both gods and men.

Orunmila, the sage of Duniyan, consulted with the gods of the land and he was told to discern a means out of Chaos. Orunmila told the people of Duniyan that the lifting up of the ancient gates of Duniyan would allow them to escape to freedom. This lifting could only be achieved if a person called Irele (translated Stoop) could be found.

Orunmila explained the task relied upon finding this Irele. She alone possessed a primordial birthright capable of tackling Chaos and lifting the ancient gates of Duniyan allowing the people to access freedom.

Orunmila further noted Irele would be known not by name, but by the person's capability to give an eternal answer to a very ancient esoteric question.

Duniyan had the option of choosing up to seven damsels to from whom one of them would at least be able to respond with an eternal answer to the very ancient esoteric question.

There was an intense search by gods and men for this personage whom Orunmila explained, would not come from the company of the gods of Duniyan but from the realm of its people.

Since this task was not to be a right of the gods, the people of Duniyan set on the search for people in the land whose attributes were perceived as close to that of the gods.

Irele after defeating Chaos

Principle 2: CHAOS – Stoop To Conquer But Look Up

These were brought to the fore in turns and with great expectation of breakthrough. They were:

Oyaya the cheerful, Afafa the conscientious, Iwa the personable, Afinju the spic and span, Bisun-Biwale the fertile, and Ewa the beautiful.

These six prominent damsels of the land with laudable virtues close to the gods were brought forward in turn and were asked the ancient esoteric question, but none was able to respond with an eternal answer.

The entire land panicked. The situation seemed forlorn. Yet Orunmila believed there was at least one more option remaining. Orunmila counselled the elders of Duniyan to extend their search across the periphery and look beyond the usual 'god-like', virtuous people.

The elders were reluctant, but as they had little option left, they despairingly acquiesced to this advice and travelled across to the periphery where they brought a little unassuming girl whom an unknown god claimed had been prepared from the onset to provide an eternal answer to the esoteric question.

The gods at Duniyan were upset with the elders of the land about such a gamble and the elders themselves could not offer an appreciable response in defence of their actions save the fact that they had few options left.

Even Orunmila, while he had counselled a search across the periphery as a last resort, was bewildered about the ineptness of the elders of Duniyan at acquiescing to the demand of an unknown god on the choice of this unassuming girl.

The girl was brought to the town square, the elders arrived, the gods of the land were summoned, Orunmila came forward and the fiery Chaos was all set with venomous trail to consume the entire Duniyan upon the failure of the girl to give an eternal answer to the esoteric question.

There was silence. The gods and elders couldn't look. Orunmila shuddered. Chaos brewed with venom and the entire Duniyan were panic-stricken, many already accepting the fate of being a food to the tyranny of Chaos.

It was a gargantuan risk; All the gods held their breath hoping that the divine gamble would pay off and not be a double 'mistake'. Fingers crossed…

Gods, men and land depended on the response of a mere peripheral girl introduced by an unknown god. There was suspense as Orunmila asked the esoteric question. Everyone, god and man alike accepted the battle had been lost because they could not understand any logic behind 'stooping to conquer'.

Upon the response of the unassuming girl, trumpets blasted, drums rolled, gongs rang. All in Duniyan assumed the battle was lost and the eternal answer to the esoteric question had been wrong.

But then, the smoke settled and behold the nine ancient gates of the land of Duniyan were gradually lifted towards an escape into newness where everything changed, and there was freshness in the air. Now Chaos was absolutely incapable of forming any attack.

By this singular act, Irele, an obscure unassuming girl out from the periphery was raised to head the profile of the gods.

The Meaning of the Story

There is much work at the margins and fringes but it is from here the work of blooming commences. When we get education and

Principle 2: CHAOS – Stoop To Conquer But Look Up

experience right, we are able to discover a plethora of Steve Jobs, Elon Musks and Barack Obamas among us (people who were once at the margin). The System ignores them at its own peril, but inclusivity and equity are a success in any domain which practices it regularly. More is required to ensure a fair, equal society.

For us to be free from the base of our situation, we must accept the state of anonymity, following established rules, learning and not being acknowledged while we develop our arts and skills in hiding and certain obscurity. We have to be content with stooping.

Stooping is not easy work. Looking up while we stoop is even tougher and harnessing the courage to conquer requires a shift in mentality which is integral to the entire Journey Back to freedom.

The answer to a breakthrough may lie where one would rather not look and as such it is not beneficial for a System to disregard and be prejudiced against anyone.

You are a champion! Believe, and work towards being the surprise treasure of your age by stooping to conquer.

This mindset, we shall discuss in the following Principle 3 - We are all wounded.

Practical suggestions towards Stooping to Conquer

1. Identify and make a note of any habit you have or any situation in which you consider demeaning.
2. Consider if this situation makes you angry, frustrated, resentful. Are you motivated enough, or have sufficient drive to want to escape?
3. Make a list of the steps you need to take and identify the sort of help you need.

Blooming Through Chaotic Times

PRINICIPLE 3.
CHAOS

WE ARE ALL WOUNDED

---

*If you have never been wounded
you will not understand how anomalies
constitute bridges to the next level of progress.*

Francis Niyi Akinola

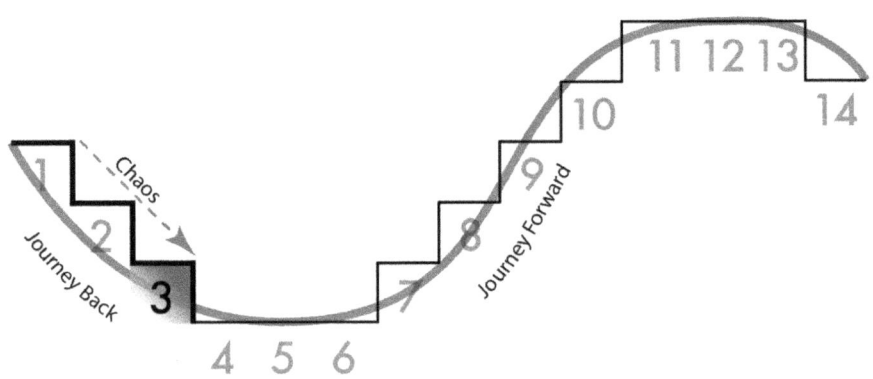

Principle 3

Principle 3: CHAOS – We Are All Wounded

Life may often be viewed as unfair. If we have any hope of getting out of the valley of the misery we experience, we have to utilise any experienced difficulty constituting a hindrance to our progress as a tool for growth.

We have to begin by developing personal responsibility before assuming criticism about others. Knowing others is intelligence, but knowing ourselves is true wisdom.

The Reality

We first have to realise the world thrives on the notion of the survival of the fittest, and, when given the space, the powerful take advantage and trample on the vulnerable. Everyone find themselves within an endless spiral of survival and prejudiced competition for whatever is at stake.

This struggle plays itself out both on the personal and global stage. We may be living in a system where the powerful few thrive at the expense of others less fortunate, but it is not useful to play the victim with inaction while blaming others for our situation, but a most effective method is to first look inwards to see how we may have contributed to the perpetuation of such injustice.

The Responsibility

We must not downscale the unfairness which goes on within every ecosystem, either on the micro or macro stage. But without a positive and forward-looking mindset which can truly and totally crush the unfairness we are experiencing, we shall be hidden within our current racist, tribal and group spiral cycle of divisions and malice, for the harm which others have caused us.

We ought to have a forward-looking mindset to crush any negativity being experienced through a method of integration and refining of ills to bring goodness through them.

This demands work and responsibility because there is little empathy for those who are down on their luck because many, upon getting to freedom, forget the struggles of when they were down. Also, many who are down are bitter and are envious of those who succeed. A positive sentiment for another person's success works better than any envy or resentment.

While being discomforted by the unfair dimension of our current circumstances, we must believe these experiences can become the food for progress with a proper understanding of our own biases in this matter.

When you are not chased, you do not learn to run, and if you do not run, you will not arrive quickly at your destination. So, run. But, if you cannot run, walk. If you cannot walk, crawl. Just keep moving by understanding this unfairness and working at your own ineptitude which contributes to the present malady.

Authenticity and integrity are very necessary in our thoughts, actions, and attitudes. We must own our feelings and work on their negativity, because, ultimately, we'll be found out for who we are.

Principle 3: CHAOS – We Are All Wounded

We have crafted systems which make it almost impossible not to be found out. Technology will not allow anyone to shed their past. The foreverness of the internet will with time, find us out and expose any hypocrisy!

Zero-sum and Positive Sum Situations

Through the cultivation of an outlook of mercy to alleviate any hate generated by a disregard of looking at situations from a victim's perspective. We do not have to play the 'zero sum' game, which results in a 'Live and Let Die' outlook of life. To move out of chaos requires developing a 'positive sum' game. 'Live and Let Live', culture since we are all in this together. Many operate from a scarcity mentality because of the chaos generated. An abundant mentality is a Positive sum perspective.

A *Zero-sum* situation is when one person's gain is exactly balanced by another person's loss. In other words, the total gains and losses in the System sum to zero. This means that if one person wins, someone else must lose. An example of a *zero-sum* game is a tennis match. If one player wins, the other player loses.

A *Positive-sum* situation is when all parties involved can benefit. In a *Positive-sum* game, the total gains are greater than the total losses. This means that if one person wins, it doesn't necessarily mean that someone else has to lose. An example of a positive-sum game is trade. When two countries engage in trade, both countries can benefit.

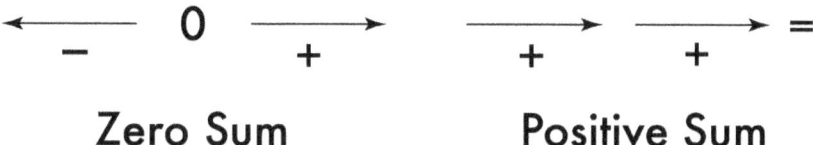

Beware of Karma

The actual evil happens if we don't look at life from the perspective of *'we are in this together'*, we can be surprisingly caught up in the karma struggle.

Karma means a person's actions have consequences which determine their future. It is the law of cause and effect that governs the universe, which means, every action that a person takes, whether good or bad, generates a reaction which will eventually come back to that person in some form or another.

We often say, *"What goes around comes around."* So, when each person sees the other person as the evil one and he is never culpable, it becomes a *zero sum* outlook where such person, rather than move forward, becomes entangled in a cyclic movement and becomes the loser.

Most Who Regard Themselves as a Hero Have Never Experienced a Battle

The mainstream media has become increasingly partisan. When we read newspapers and watch TV, it is easy to form an opinion.

The media rummages for scandals and thrives on a good guy versus bad guy narrative which could shatter a lifelong reputation in an instant. The more the audience shares their views, the more the cash in their pockets.

Sometimes we use a sledge hammer to kill an ant. A single moment of error can destroy a life-built reputation. Public condemnations are rife and ruthless, bolstered by social and print media. Beneath these lurk frailty and fragility, insufficiency and weakness, plus a deep vulnerability of our humanity which we have all experienced or are now experiencing.

Principle 3: CHAOS – We Are All Wounded

The Rise and Rise of Big Brother

We have built a culture or system where it is difficult to balance actions with ethics and there are lots of hypocrisy in the middle. The football VAR scenario where nothing escapes justice (though justice could still be amiss) is a good analogy of how our mode of judgement could be ruthless even while being fair.

We have an ethical responsibility to confront our own flaws, rather than excuse ourselves while condemning others. Addressing this would increase our moral benchmark. As Paulo Coelho says, *"If you want to be successful you must respect one rule: never lie to yourself."*

We are all wounded, to varying degrees. If we fail to look inward to realize our common woundedness, the tide could change and a hero of today could easily become a villain of tomorrow. That is what karma does to the person who lives a *zero sum* narrative.

How to Deal with Scandal?

We, of course, should not excuse evil. We know that where law ends, tyranny begins; without personal discipline and maintaining a social rule of law, unity cannot be sustained, because, universal laws alone cannot sustain any progress.

What is wrong needs to be dealt with, but what becomes disturbing is our expertise at condemnation based on the torrent of limited information which we acquire from TV, newspapers, and social media.

We continue to ruthlessly and mercilessly condemn the many scandals in the media but when our personal 'chickens come home to roost', we may then realize how spontaneous condemnation of evil is as evil as the act.

Without any tolerance in our correctional process, we will all, at some point be culprits of ruthless condemnation. We must continually find means of introducing compassion into our judicial system because, ultimately, we are all complicit in anomalies.

It is not enough to look at the corruption and evils of institutions. If you have not been able to journey into the depth and experienced the capability and potential of your own capacity for evils, you are not yet able to transcend to the next level of the journey.

An acknowledgement of our collective woundedness is more beneficial than any isolated creativity. We are not to run away from weakness and vulnerabilities, rather, we must be patient with ourselves and work towards integrating them.

Integrating our Shadow

Authenticity is what sets us free, yet in a world where many hide under hypocritical cloaks, authenticity wavers and everyone fails under this moral challenge. We cannot *'fake it till we make it'* as popular culture suggests. We need to have a means of 'integrating our shadow'.

Integrating one's shadow is a process of becoming more aware of and accepting the parts of oneself that are often hidden or repressed.

The first step is to identify the parts of ourselves we tend to hide or repress (our shadow). These can be traits, emotions, or experiences we judge as negative, shameful or unacceptable.

Once we have identified our shadow, it is important to acknowledge it. We do not have to like or approve of these parts of ourselves only acknowledge and accept.

We can then take time to reflect on the origins of our shadow, and how it has affected our life. We can consider how it has influenced our behaviours, relationships and decisions.

Once we stop trying to hide, deny or repress our shadow and consciously acknowledge it we need to start practicing self-compassion. As it is often said, charity begins at home and here home is our inner self.

The problem lies with self-awareness and laziness. Integrating one's shadow is a work and can be emotionally taxing, this is why many ignore this and prefer to look outside to condemn everybody else. The journey may start by blaming others, but when we acknowledge blame in ourselves we begin real healing.

When we can eventually blame no one yet still accept responsibility; when we refuse to judge indiscriminately and agree not to be influenced, we are making progress. This attitude will be of great help during the Journey Forward, when we become a success within certain endeavour, as the tide turns we change from the judge to the judged.

By becoming more aware of and accepting our shadow, we can live a more authentic and fulfilling life, aware of our biases which leads us towards expanding on wrongdoings.

Biases

I recently got caught jumping the red traffic light and I was put on a traffic training course which greatly benefited me. From there I learnt about three biases which make us do the wrong things until we are eventually found out:

First is **Optimism Bias**: A certain feeling which convinces us that we can always get away with things by obeying the 11th commandment, *'Do not be caught'*. Every day is for the thief, one day is for the owner. It takes a little mistake, an incorrect decision to be found out and pay for all past misdeeds.

The second is called **What Worked Bias**. The fact something is laudable today does not mean it will always be so. You may be the jailer today and for the same cause, you can turn into the criminal. Life moves and justice is not static.

The third is called **Self Enhancement Bias**. We forget the things which we do badly and we refuse to seek a redress towards improvement; we become complacent at being wrong.

We need to master these biases, and from it, we can see how we are all susceptible to these human flaws. How we are all wounded. This poem called Judge Softly by Mary T. Lathrap echoes this well:

Judge Softly
Pray don't find fault with the man who limps
or stumbles along the road,
unless you have worn the shoes he wears
or struggled beneath his load.
There may be tacks in his shoes that hurt,
though hidden away from view,
or the burden he bears, placed on your back
might cause you to stumble too.
Don't sneer at the man who's down today
unless you have felt the blow
that caused his fall or felt the shame
that only the fallen know.
You may be strong, but still the blows
that were his if dealt to you,
in the selfsame way, at the selfsame time,
might cause you to stagger too.
Don't be too harsh with the man who sins
or pelt him with word or stone,
unless you are sure, yea, doubly sure,
that you have no sins of your own –

Principle 3: CHAOS – We Are All Wounded

*For you know perhaps if the tempter's voice
should whisper as softly to you
as it did to him when he went astray,
it might cause you to stumble too.*

To have not experienced a struggle or vulnerability of the accused opens one up to an improper judgement and an unconscious bias about the accused, it causes the accuser to be prone to judgement.

The Professor and The Village Boy

This situation can be related to this funny story about an anthropology professor who was crossing a river in a boat paddled by a young boy in an African village in a bid to research his next book.

The journey was slow, and the boat boy was silent. Before long the professor became restless and asked the boy "Tell me young man," he says, "Do you know Biology?

The boy responded, 'Oga (meaning: master), I no know Biology o'.

The professor was alarmed and puzzled, he told the boy: 'You do not understand Biology and you are in this jungle all alone? A quarter of your life is already wasted then.

The boy felt ashamed and sorry for his state, before long the professor interjected again: 'Young man, working in this sort of environment puts you in an acute predicament without knowledge. Do you know anything about, geology, ecology or epidemiology at all?

The boy felt ashamed but decided to be truthful, he responded 'Oga, I no know Geology, Ecology or Epidemiology'.

'What?!' The professor shouted surprisingly, doing such a job in such an environment, without this basic knowledge means half of your life is gone. Your illiteracy will kill you within an ecosystem such as this'. The young boy was sorry for his state but he continued to paddle the boat awkwardly along.

An hour later, the boat sprung a leak and started to sink. The professor began to panic and the young boy was surprised about his agitation. He asked 'Oga, why you dey fear (why are you scared). Do you know about Swimology?

The professor, after some clarifications about what 'Swimology' meant, confessed that he could not swim; and the boy said,

'Oga, without Swimology, there is no escapology from crocodiolgy and you go drownology. E be like say the whole of your life done go!'

The boy jumped into the river and began to swim across the shore leaving the professor scared for his life in the boat.

We may be the judge (the professor) of a matter today, but there may be one little thing which may be lacking, upon which our progress and existence may depend.

The Professor and The Village Boy

Principle 3: CHAOS – We Are All Wounded

As narrated in the story *'Where Freedom Lies'*, in Principle 2: Stoop to conquer but look up, a System's survival hinges on the skills or 'know-how' of an unassuming person on the periphery. If the people of Duniyan had followed their biases their fate would have been sealed. Our biases often blind us in the discovery of opportunities around us.

Balancing Justice and Mercy

There are many difficult questions we ask, all with complex answers. For instance, to what extent should justice be tempered by mercy? In the age of knowledge, how beneficial would it be to express our vulnerabilities without public condemnation?

To what extent is our environment receptive and understanding of the fact that we do not thrive by eliminating vulnerabilities but through their authentic integration?

Authentic integration with value for excellence is needed to develop a more coherent culture where we can judge flaws through an authentic outlook and mindset of mercy. If we cannot do this, I doubt if any of us would coherently journey out of the chaos to which we are subjected.

Our wounds are our source of progress and we should be careful of promoting exclusion and inequality in the System. It is already a warped System which continually disfavours the already disfavoured.

When we understand the concept 'we are all wounded', we shall then begin to gain the consistency to move on through our Journey Back in order to Journey Forward.

Practical Suggestions to heal our Woundedness

1. Stand in front of the mirror. Look at yourself in the mirror, view and acknowledge your woundedness.
2. Think of someone who has hurt you and make efforts to forgive and heal.
3. Can you take practical steps to contact such person? Remember to be considerate of how they may feel, they may still feel wounded and unresponsive to any advances you wish to make.

COHERENCE

The Coherence Principles (4-7)

*These Principles address the necessity of discipline
and patient forbearance, attitude and practices
to foster breakthroughs and success
in the midst of ordeals.*

PRINCIPLE 4. COHERENCE - CONSISTENCY IS KEY

Passion with persistence is what genius is about.

Angela Lee Duckworth

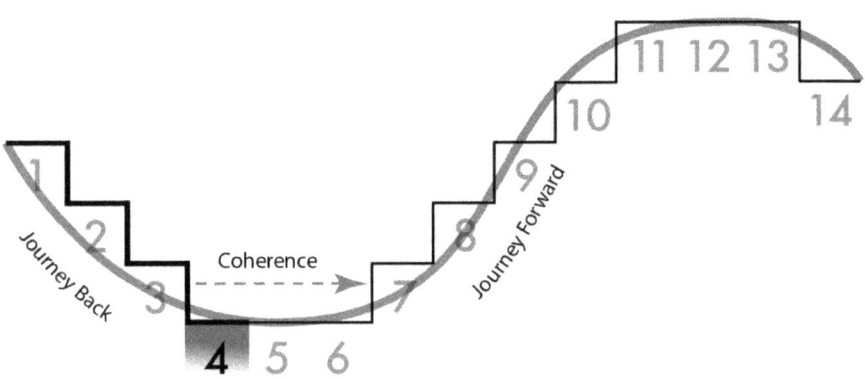

Principle 4

The man who starts early enough has an advantage over anyone who procrastinates. You must set forth at dawn. There is no short cut, no magic bullet, no secret formula or quick fix to success or as I like to say to 'blooming' in life.

Sure, there are the very minorities who win lotteries, but if you have an aversion to work, discipline and commitment, even if you win the lottery (the probability for winning the UK lottery, is 1 in 292,201,338) you may still not get out of the downward spiral without a disciplined attitude and mentality.

The reality is, good things take time to build and there is no other time to start but now!

I believe in luck and miracles, but these themselves are unpredictable. The best certainty is to repeat something over and over then we can hope to excel.

We've observed life is fragile, but consistency, discipline and practice around an interest is the best proof we have of success after the development of an ideal. This gives us our fourth Principle - Consistency is Key.

To be thoroughly successful, you must have a slow and formidable endeavour. Those who are simply lucky at becoming successful often become unlucky as they crash out, if they do not build on their luck and learn discipline to keep it.

Some Observations on Consistency

Mark Manson, American author, said, *"People want to start their own business or become financially independent. But you don't end up a successful entrepreneur unless you find a way to love the risk, the uncertainty, the repeated failures, and working insane hours on something you have no idea whether will be successful or not."*

What Manson said of business is also relevant to most life's endeavours. Naval Ravikant once said: *"A fit body, a calm mind, a house full of love. These things cannot be bought - they must be earned"*. By 'earning', he meant they must be worked at through self-discipline.

We have to spend enough time at something in order to master it and be good at it, time is a huge factor. Success is the sum of small efforts - repeated day in, day out, but there has to be a time tolerance for error corrections and iterations.

No one would notice you unless you are unique, and to be unique, you must have devoted long time at practice. The years of which only the victor knows.

Tryon Edwards observed the fruit of consistency as this, *"Any act often repeated soon forms a habit; and habit allowed, steady gains in strength, at first it may be but as a spider's web, easily broken through, but if not resisted it soon binds us with chains of steel."*

You've heard it said, *'Time is money'*, but time is more valuable than money, since it cannot be retrieved. Money lost can be recouped, but time wasted is gone with the wind, forever. So, a wise person guards and spends his time wisely, even more than he does his money.

Principle 4: COHERENCE – Consistency is Key

Another idiom is, *'Practice makes perfect.'* You are only strong to the extent at which you allow yourself to be resolutely determined; not to get discouraged, not to give up.

Consistency, grit, endurance and dedication are keys to the successes we see in the world. We become expert at something when we are able to dedicate time, energy and effort to it.

Helen Keller once said, *"Do not think of today's failures, but of the success that may come tomorrow. You have set yourselves a difficult task, but you will succeed if you persevere, and you will find joy in overcoming obstacles. Remember, no effort that we make to attain something beautiful is ever lost."*

Strive to Follow Your Interests and Find Meaning

It is important to be trained in an area that we are interested in so that when routine comes, we are able to persist. We can be considered twice lucky when we have an interest and a natural ability in a particular skill; and three times as lucky if we understand with these, training and natural ability, the capability of maintaining a disciplined consistency, which I expand on in this principle. You do not become a genius through sloth; excellence comes through persistence.

Having said this, I do agree that innate skill and talent does help success, however a person who is persistent at an interest will ultimately outstrip someone who has talent but no drive. Passion with persistence is what genius is about.

The Persistent Boy who Trumped my Skill

Here is a personal story to emphasise the case of how consistency, resilience and determination can conquer skill and complacency.

When I was in Year 2 in high school, I was top of the sprint team among my group (Intermediate height). It was a glorious period for me in high school and, ultimately, one of the most humiliating. I simply turned up on sprint lanes and took winning for granted. There was a boy in a lower class, Waidi Biobaku (I can't forget his name) who eventually made me give up a career in sprint.

He always came second at sprints on our sports days while I basked in the euphoria of my success and popularity. Though I had a natural talent for sprint and it came at no cost to me, I took this winning as a given.

Now Waidi, during holiday breaks and after school, would devote himself to practice, he joined the athletics club at the stadium and as I learnt later, he was determined to squash my popularity and come out on top. I didn't see Waidi as a threat because, though he came in 2nd, I always won by a wide margin.

The following sports year I took my winning as a given, but was scandalously humiliated when Waidi started to trump me at sprints by an equally wide margin. Now, I realise how in life, devotion, attentiveness and practice beats natural talents. I would love to speak to my naive and complacent younger self!

The Need to Align Roles to Innate Talents

In order to boost success through consistency, it is necessary to align talents and innate abilities to personal interest. There is always the temptation for parents, governments or organisations to force their wards into culturally acceptable or desired roles.

It is necessary for a System to build and train for expertise, but in the long run, it would be a much safer bet to ensure individual roles are geared towards interest and ability.

Principle 4: COHERENCE – Consistency is Key

A cultural pushing into an area of life which does not come naturally or one which is not of personal interest to an individual, becomes an invitation to dealing with malice, resentment and even mental illness.

The Persistent Discipline to Tarry

Many become discouraged and give up at the slightest inconvenience of failure. An African proverb says, *'If the eye is patient and persistent enough, it shall behold the nose.'* Without 'doing', there will be no change, and without our changing, nothing will change!

We may also be forced into circumstances where we may have to wait, but as Ray Davis says *"Patience is not passive waiting. Patience is active acceptance of the process required to attain your goals and dreams."*

To do in spite of being forced to be still, to hold together when everyone else would fall apart, that is true strength.

Some Examples of Persistence:

Michael Jordan, the renowned American Basketball player recounted of his career, he said, *'I've missed over 9000 shots in my career, I've lost almost 300 games. 26 times I've been trusted to take the game's winning shot and missed. I've failed over and over and over again in my life. And that is why I succeed.'*

Whenever I was working out and got tired and figured I ought to stop, I'd close my eyes and see that list in the locker room without my name on it, and that usually got me going again."

It is this internal drive which breeds persistence and it is also echoed by Thomas Edison, the light bulb inventor, when he is quoted as saying, *"Our greatest weakness lies in giving up. The most certain way to succeed is always to try just one more time."* and *"Many of life's failures are people who did not realize how close they were to success when they gave up."*

Abraham Lincoln is a tale of exemplary resilience in success. In business, Lincoln failed twice, as a politician he lost eight elections and he suffered a nervous break-down, and yet he's arguably the best American president ever.

A personal story of how naturally the years in the dark of perseverance can ultimately benefit the subject is my driving story.

Lincoln, Jordan and Edison

My Personal Story of Resilience

I'd never had a more horrible story of failure as my driving experience. It began when my wife was pregnant with our second child and I was desperate to learn to drive.

Principle 4: COHERENCE – Consistency is Key

Anyone who's taken driving exams in London will tell you how tough it is to pass, but my own driving failure in the midst was exceptional.

I went through many driving lessons and examinations without success, this got increasingly frustrating until I met with Dave my last driving instructor.

Dave, unlike my other driving instructors told me, *"I'd get you out there driving in the shortest possible time but you've got to agree to my terms."*

I asked, *"What are your terms?"* He explained, first, unlike other driving instructors who come around to pick me up, I had to commute 12 miles to his destination.

Then, he told me to dump manual driving, which I was adamant on learning, and told me to start on automatic driving, which was more expensive, but simpler to manoeuvre.

Dave's method of teaching was straightforward. He was not interested in making me an expert at driving, he rather taught me simple tricks which would give me confidence on the road.

I took my 9th driving exam while I was with Dave and I failed by a very narrow point, instead of the usual waiting for 3 months which other drivers do, I discovered from Dave how one could book immediately for another driving test.

This happened a few weeks later and on the 18th October (I won't forget that day) I passed at last. My third child was now two years old. Better late than never.

After I eventually passed my driving exam, on my 10th attempt, Dave said something counter-cultural to my understanding of success. He said, *"You will have a great success story to tell your kids."*

Initially, it was unclear to me what he meant (I did not catch the 'success' element until after reflecting on his comment) Nigerian Dads usually don't persistently fail at skills and tell their children. To their kids, they are always 'top of their class'!

Now, when I would hire people in business, I prefer to listen to histories of failures and persistence rather than those of continual success. Grit is what ultimately distinguishes success from failures.

Grit was what Rocky Balboa counselled his son about in the legendary movie 'Rocky'.

He told his son :

"Let me tell you something you already know. The world ain't all sunshine and rainbows. It's a very mean and nasty place and I don't care how tough you are it will beat you to your knees and keep you there permanently if you let it. You, me, or nobody is gonna hit as hard as life. But it ain't about how hard you're hit. It's about how hard you can get hit and keep moving forward. How much you can take and keep moving forward. That's how winning is done!

Now if you know what you're worth then go out and get what you're worth. But ya gotta be willing to take the hits, and not pointing fingers saying you ain't where you wanna be because of him, or her, or anybody! Cowards do that and that ain't you! You're better than that!"

Success is not about never failing; it is about the ability to pick oneself up when one fails.

Principle 4: COHERENCE – Consistency is Key

Between Faithful Consistency and Foolish Time-Wasting

The viewpoint is, how do we differentiate between faithful consistency and situations demanding changes unto other experiences?

As Albert Einstein would say, *"The definition of insanity is doing the same thing over and over again and expecting a different result."* The question thus arises of what the option of not giving up would entail and what the actual period to consider exiting an endeavour portend.

The clue may lie in the strength of our purpose. *Friedrich Nietzsche said, "If you have a why strong enough, you would bear almost any how."* For me, the necessity to transport my family around the country was my strong 'why'. I had very little alternative otherwise. It was this resolve which wouldn't let me give up and it was what eventually drove me to success at driving a car.

I've now driven for many years and so far without a single accidental scratch (fingers crossed). The years of driving and failing tests has accumulated into building expertise at driving such that I could say I've recouped the money spent in lessons from a no accident existence.

Often, life is more an art than science, it takes a lot of self-awareness and deep resolve to develop the sense of what and where one's commitments should be directed, as such, the prayer by Reinhold Niebuhr popularised by the Alcoholics Anonymous, may be applicable,

"God grant me the serenity to accept the things I cannot change, courage to change the things I can and wisdom to know the difference."

To know whether to hold on or to let go is part of self-awareness and self-actualisation, something we need to learn.

Between Passion and Subsistence

In economic terms, this lack of clarity about letting go or holding on often happens because of tension between the building of an innate passion and the need to maintain subsistence through an activity which is not of interest to the person.

The gap between passion and subsistence lies in the wait. To thrive demands a need to balance an innate purpose with a forced demand by the System.

For instance, in the working world, the industrial revolution has compelled many out of their innate 'whys' into generalised 'hows' as mostly defined by the System. There is certain disenfranchisement between personal purpose and career specialisations.

However, the tide may be turning back again as many people are once more discovering a merger between their 'whys' and 'hows'. They are increasingly deciding the trajectory of their life. This is the reason why 'working from home' is becoming a norm.

The Power of Persistence

When we discover our 'whys', it is difficult to give it up for mediocrity. Paul Romer noticed how people are reasonably good at estimating how things add up, but not how things can create compound benefit. When people realise the power in the geometric progression (the compound - 1,2,4,8, 16 etc), rather than the arithmetic progression (the adding up - 1,2,3,4 etc), giving up may not be as rife.

Principle 4: COHERENCE – Consistency is Key

This compound progression applies to every aspect of life; financial, habits, and more so, in the building of people and organisations.

I'm often surprised for instance, how St Thomas Aquinas Chaplaincy (STAC) Alumni, a little group of friends which I belong to from Nigeria, has gradually transformed itself from a little group set up by college friends, now into a global organization through the shared consistency of its respective leaders. It is because they add a strong 'why'.

Authentic Community building, to the extent of being global demands great patience and persistence. On the other hand, talking about people, one huge anomaly of our age is our short attention span. Many fail because they get out too soon. They randomly change their plans because they don't have the discipline to follow through.

Practice makes perfect as this Principle - Consistency is Key reminds us. Nothing is fun until one is good at it, and leaving too soon disrupts that.

Some Steps Towards Consistency

Here is some advice towards becoming consistent and thereby achieving expertise and thus bloom out of chaos:

The primary duty is to find a passion, a meaningful purpose in your passion; discover something to love while you do it irrespective of any underlying reward. Make your work a play and do it over and over.

In our age where there is no shortage of information and where knowledge is abundant, what would differentiate us from the pack is to develop a calling, to discover a passion, purpose and persistence which sets us apart from the pack and enable us to build a specific knowledge which is unique to us.

The SMART Objectives framework described earlier in the first Principle will aid the creation of a schedule around our resolve and plans.

Also, when you take a creative approach make sure to record, monitor and evaluate yourself. To be consistent you have to ensure you recognise when you don't reach the standards and goals that you've set. Reward yourself when you get something done; small rewards help keep you motivated throughout the process.

Working hard is important but working 'smart' trumps working hard. The beginning of working smart is by setting up the SMART process for your purpose.

Plan for success, and don't beat yourself up if you make a mistake along the way. Keep going if you make a mistake.

Consistency doesn't mean that you are working all of the time. Learn to take time off to recharge and as a last resort know when your resolve is not being fruitful, have an exit strategy.

On the whole, Don't Quit. Grit ultimately trumps capacity, and as Winston Churchill remarked, *"Continuous effort - not strength or intelligence - is the key to unlocking our potential."*

While Ivan Misner advocates, *"Don't do 100 things three times, do three things 100 times. The best way to persecute your progress is not to engage, not to work."*

Anyone who finds more excitement in the Journey than the destination is a most self-actualised person.

In the 1920s, Edgar A. Guest wrote the inspirational poem, *Don't Quit.*

Principle 4: COHERENCE – Consistency is Key

Don't Quit

When things go wrong, as they sometimes will,
When the road you're trudging seems all uphill,
When the funds are low but the debts are high,
And you want to smile but you have to sigh,
When care is pressing you down a bit,
Rest if you must, but don't you quit.
Life is strange with its twists and turns,
As every one of us sometimes learns,
And many failures turn about,
When we might have won had we stuck it out.
Don't give up though the pace seems slow –
You may succeed with another blow.
Success is failure turned inside out –
The silver tint of the clouds of doubt,
You can never tell how close you are,
It may be near when it seems so far;
So stick to the fight when you're hardest hit –
It's when things seem worst that you must not quit.
Keep walking and don't quit,
for if we persevere, after darkness comes dawn
and the air when set in motion becomes wind,
but 'You must set forth at Dawn'.

I have seen with this mastery of consistency, there is no dusk, your dawn starts with your resolve and it continues along the journey ever new and fresh as the dawn.

There are attributes needed to maintain consistency. These attributes shall be further expanded as we Journey to the next Principle.

Practical Suggestions Towards Consistency

1. Draw out a 30-day consistency chart on something you have to do and stick to it.
2. Track and record the progress of your consistency chart daily.
3. Analyse this chart on a frequent basis and see what progress you are making.
4. Reward yourself for your successes.

PRINCIPLE 5.
COHERENCE - HOPE WITH COURAGE AND INTEGRITY

Fortune favours the bold.

Terence (c. 190-159 B.C.)

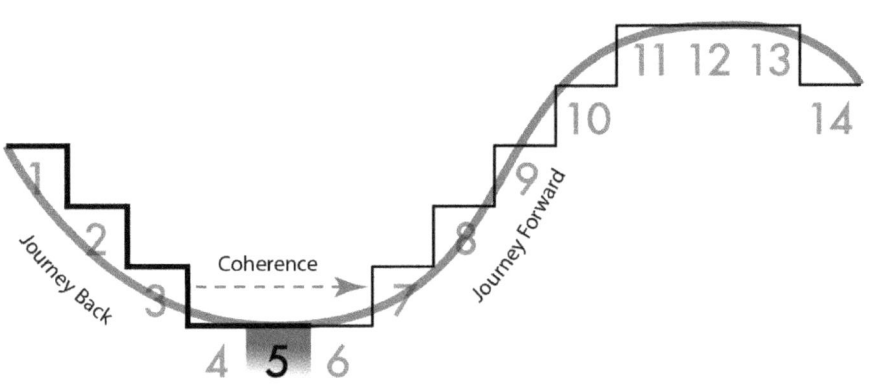

Principle 5

Principle 5: COHERENCE – Hope with Courage and Integrity

The real tragedy of our age is the damage of hope. Hope, which is the great motivator of life and civilisation has been reduced to a passing emotion. In spite of the many books written about the need to hope and to stay resilient, few people are able to utilise hope appropriately because they do not accompany hope with courage and integrity.

Hope is more than just optimism because hope can be subtly killed when we have an optimism which is irrational, that is, one which is unwilling to be realistic about the state of things and draw an appropriate action towards tackling specific difficulties. When one is in a challenging situation, to live in unrealistic hope creates a double calamity.

How Can You Be Sure You Are Actively Waiting?

The bedrock of all progress is not the denial of chaos, as seen in our time. Catastrophes happen, which can be fatal and unbearable, but we should not be engrossed by them.

Do not stay too long listening to the news which thrives from negativity, this leads to hopelessness, mental trauma and ultimately death. This may be why so many suffer from neurosis and anxiety.

The tool here is in active and realistic hope. The ability to stay in a domain of stress in order to impact it positively is a choice and commitment (this is active waiting) which has been described as closer to wisdom than mere informational knowledge.

Propaganda of False Hope

While we should watch against negative news and doomsday propaganda, we should also be watchful of those who are not realistic and create false hopes.

Growing up in Nigeria, there was a rave of 'prosperity pastors' who bought into the psyche of the masses by preaching an irrational hope without responsibilities, with little or no delay of gratification.

They had huge followings, especially among the young and the poor, because apart from the sweetness of their rhetoric, such messages were more appealing to the heart despite their falsehood.

The same cord rings in the entitled world of modern materialism as the media portray a bliss with little sense of duty. If we buckle out of a crisis in the face of some little difficulties, how would we then be wise?

The real evil is neither ethics nor morals, but living in their lies and denial. We lie and deny because we see no way out of our faults and weaknesses.

The Audacity of Hope

Acts of courage create hope and there is nothing more essential to the human spirit than hope. As Paulo Coelho clearly states, *"Tenacious hope achieves anything, and when you want something, all the universe conspires in helping you to achieve it."*

Principle 5: COHERENCE – Hope with Courage and Integrity

Hope has to do with patience, and patience profits, for good things often come to those who can wait. Real hope breaks us from the shackles of mediocrity, it forges us on, in spite of limiting obstacles. Authentic hope is rational and it does not fail.

Often, we feel the backward impact of the Journey Back, which seem to outweigh the positive prospect which going through our experiences promises, but it is necessary to be optimistic and to align ourselves within the frequency of a holistic positive trajectory of life.

On the Need for Courage

If there is anything that can beat chaos, it is hope and perseverance. Hope is in a dogged 'why' which uses courage and truth to break off the shackles imposed by chaos.

It is unlikely anything will be handed over to you on a platter (it is not to your benefit if you take an easy route, as it is likely you will not value it and will misuse it). We have to dare. Fortune favours the bold and Grit trumps Power.

But, while courage is a great virtue, integrity is the hallmark of success in any endeavour. Hope, courage and integrity must go hand in hand, and anyone without these will have no progress in the Journey.

The Odyssey: A Great Example of Courage

The Odyssey is one of literature's most enduring stories based on the adventures of Odysseus, King of Ithaca, and his Journey Back after the Trojan War. It is a classic story of how hope can utilise courage and integrity to inspire freedom.

At the start of the story, we find Odysseus stranded on an island after the Trojan War ended. He longed to return home to his wife, Penelope, and their young son, Telemachus, but the journey would not be an easy one.

He experienced a Journey Back which lasted for ten years, during which he encountered and overcame incredible obstacles and perils. The story teaches us many valuable lessons about perseverance, courage, resourcefulness, loyalty, humility, self-control, and the importance of home and family.

These lessons remain just as relevant today as they were when first written, thousands of years ago. They serve as an inspiration to all who seek to overcome challenges and achieve their goals.

Odysseus hope was spurred by his purpose: his dogged desire to reunite with Penelope his wife and Telemachus his son. He displayed such enviable simplicity and courage in spite of obvious weaknesses and helplessness in the face of 'Power'. Rather than denying his weakness, he owned it and never excused it at resisting the lures of Calypso and admitted he needed the assistance of the gods in order to be rescued. Courage is not an absence of weakness; it is about acting in spite of one's weakness.

He experienced the temptations to lust and power with his encounter with the beautiful goddess Calypso who had fallen deeply in love with him. In spite of a promise of immortality from Calypso he refused to let go of his chief purpose.

He displayed great courage within his Journey Back home. He did not lose hope when he was shipwrecked and displayed courage by dragging his friend forcefully back to the ship by force from lotus-eaters who had given his men fruits that caused them to forget their homecoming.

Knowing he had a mission to fulfil, when his twelve ships were driven off course by storms and they landed on an

Principle 5: COHERENCE – Hope with Courage and Integrity

uninhabited island, and they were in danger of being murdered by Polyphemus the monster, he showed craft and bravery by courageously rescuing his men from the cave.

Odysseus was also humble enough to realise he needed help. He was mindful, attentive and willing to learn. For instance he listens to instruction and delayed his gratification by not eating the sacred livestock of Helios on the Island of Thracia, a disobedience which caused the loss of his entire crew.

Odysseus' Temptation

On Addictions

A large part of our battle during the Journey Back would be with the self. Addictions abound in our age and almost no one is bereft entirely of them. Remember: we are all wounded.

Addictions can be of many natures, alcohol, drugs (including nicotine, opioids, stimulants, etc.), gambling, video games, social media, pornography, food, sex: even some not-so-apparent addictions like shopping, eating disorders, hoarding, body modifications, compulsive lying, or being busy. These addictions are the modern-day Circes, Calypsos, Poseidon, Sirens and Scyllas, which we have to battle in our personal odyssey towards realising our goals and fulfilling our purpose.

The craving for these addictions, often starting from the desire to be accepted by our peers, can create compromises and swerve us from our goals as they seek to pull us from the beam of our vision. Participation in them creates dopamine in our brain, which could distract us from real purpose, achievement and real fulfilment, keeping us a slave of desires and pawns of the System.

Tackling Addictions

Addiction is a complex issue, and overcoming it can be challenging. However, like Odysseus, it may be a long Journey Back home, but denial is equally as defeating as giving up hope of overcoming addiction. With the right mindset, tools, and support, it is possible.

The first step in overcoming an addiction is to admit that there is a problem. Denial can prevent someone from seeking help and making progress. We touched on this in Principle 3.

Integrity begins with being realistic about the situation, and it is integrity such as this, combined with courage, which creates a willingness to hope.

We may be looking forward to achieving a purpose, but overcoming addiction is a goal within a purpose and it is worth treating it as such. Having a goal, developing a plan for how to

Principle 5: COHERENCE – Hope with Courage and Integrity

cope with cravings and setbacks can help one to stay motivated and focused amidst the chaos of addiction.

It is also crucial to have a support system which can provide encouragement, accountability, and guidance. This can be family, friends, a community organization, or a professional counsellor or support group.

This is what we aim towards at Framat and ARC and You: supporting individuals through difficult struggles in their lives, relationships and careers.

Through these organisations, we have assisted many with training, development of healthy alternatives and signposting individuals to further necessary help in their Journey Back struggles: leading towards breakthrough into their individual Journey Forward.

Regarding tackling addictions, avoiding triggers, which can lead to relapse, may be hard but it is crucial in this game. This may involve avoiding certain people, places, or situations that are associated with the addiction.

We may fail and be disappointed with ourselves over and over, but we are all in this wounded game, and quitting in the struggle of life would simply widen the gulf on the Journey.

Overcoming an addiction is a process, it takes time, patience, and perseverance. With the right mindset, tools, and support, it is possible to break free from these addictions and live a fulfilling life. Courage, hope and integrity are crucial in our salvation.

Lessons from Odysseus

The Odysseus saga echoes the ordeals which we as individuals would have to master towards the Journey Back to freedom. We shall have to encounter the powers that be who knowingly or unknowingly seek to deter our progress, it is useless to whine and whinge.

Life to a certain degree is as ruthless as the saga of Odysseus and it will take hope, courage, integrity, grit, tact and drive to achieve your purpose and fulfil your destiny.

In Conclusion

Do not allow yourself simply to be subservient to the System without having control of your desires and aspirations.

Many are struggling for similar resources that you are aiming for, and because everyone wants what you want, they can choose to maim and destroy in the process. But, in order for you to progress in this Journey to freedom, look at reality from a positive mindset and have this dogged belief that your turn will come and, when it comes, it shall abound in a most interesting and lasting manner.

We need to revert to a knowledge where we step back from the rat race, where we place emphasis on community values, friendship, mental and physical well-being of everyone.

There is no redemption in violence though. The courage of hope is what brings renewal.

Practical Suggestions for Sustaining Hope with Courage and Integrity

1. List three experiences which would warrant you moving beyond your comfort zone.
2. List three benefits which you would profit from going beyond your comfort zone.
3. Talk about this to someone in order to foster accountability.

PRINCIPLE 6. COHERENCE – MEMORY IS THE VEHICLE OUT OF CHAOS

*Grief can bring back the dead to life.
The real misfortune is forgetfulness and neglect.*

Francis Niyi Akinola

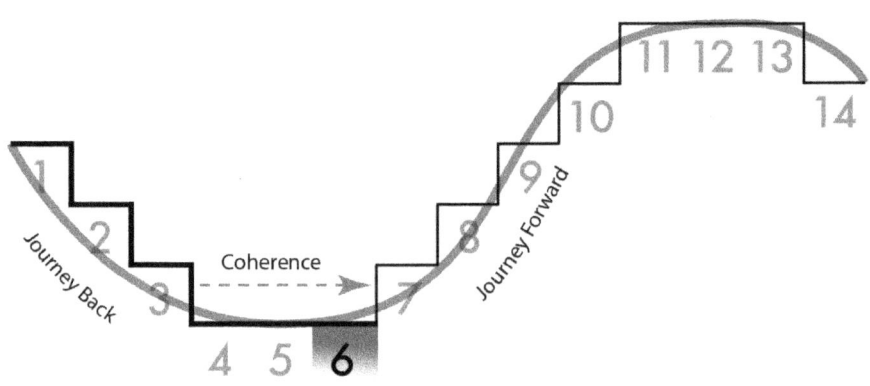

Principle 6

Principle 6: COHERENCE – Memory is the Vehicle out of Chaos

Making a Journey Back in order to bloom forward entails facing uncomfortable demons and ghosts which we each meet in our individual circumstances. Looking after yourself and keeping a positive attitude during these circumstances are avenues towards a successful life and freedom. This chapter investigates memory and how it helps us move forward.

Refusing the temptation to quit through discouraging sentiments such as boredom, loneliness, and the feeling of our insufficiencies and nothingness is a hallmark for success.

To bloom out of any chaotic circumstance, it is necessary to dare to look where we would rather not and to go where we are not ready to go. It is within these spaces we find clues to what we seek. We have to be loyal to our human experience in order not to fall short.

Blooming out from Grief

The essence of existence is found in the attitude we take towards unavoidable suffering.

One of many devastating experiences of the Journey Back is the loss of something dear, either of loved ones, a position or job. Many can identify with this experience. Grief is the inevitable consequence of what we would rather be spared of.

Grief forces us into dark spaces where we can understand our powerlessness in the face of change, but it can be where we find potential. Immense energy is found in sorrow which is often untapped because few dare look when grief strikes.

Memory is the Vehicle out of Grief

Using Memory to Discover Purpose

We would like to avoid pain, but through this pain, maturity grows and meaning can be obtained from what was a seeming meaningless experience. This is where we learn.

You may be familiar with the phrase, *'No cross, no crown'*, we can see, the cross is the grief and crown is a strong purpose which nothing can stop. This is not easily come by.

Grief enables purpose: without death, there is no rebirth. Both death and grief are important moments of becoming.

This grief does not only come about through bereavement. We undergo a great many slow deaths every time, and I believe the slowness of dying in everyday affairs can be worse than the suddenness of death itself.

Principle 6: COHERENCE – Memory is the Vehicle out of Chaos

By daring to tap into our harrowing experiences, and with a right attitude, we can produce glorious consequences within a Journey Back. How do we do this you may ask? Through memory.

Grief is a school and memory is the teacher. 'Remembering', should ultimately give reality a boost, developing in individuals, the desire, meaning and accomplishment which in ordinary circumstances they would never achieve.

Using Memory to Heal

Nothing should be forgotten. When we have the audacity to use memory to hope, everything can be redeemed. No true sage counsels forgetfulness. Through memory we can have a positive effect, so we should embrace the journey through grief and thus utilise the process towards healing.

We should hold on, but not too much. We should let go, but not too much, the philosopher Rumi said, *'Life is found between the balance of holding on and letting go.'* It is within this balance that we find the utility of a memory which heals.

Memory may be painful, but when it is hurting and we dare to look and wait, we are undergoing the process of healing ourselves and the painful past. This way we can lay a solid foundation towards building a new and glorious future.

Memory is not only found in grief, it is also discovered from lesson learnt, either from an error or from work. The important thing is to use our memories and tap into the expended energy.

The Discipline from Memory

The discipline is not to take things for granted and to be patient while seeking meaning from chaos. I must say this is not an easy task.

I was only ten years old when I lost my mom. Such experience at an early age made life take a dramatic turn for me and this early setback, through thick and thin, has integrally defined what I have become today.

A Personal Memory Tale

There is a saying, *'A dead mom never really sleeps'*, and as George Elliot said, *"Our dead are never dead to us until we have forgotten them."* This has been my experience of growing from the chaos of bereavement, down to the dogged refusal by my siblings and myself to forget our mom.

We were compelled by memory, or was it the depth of pain and loss which triggered a lingering memory? All I can say is that my mom's memory became an integral part of our existence, even from our early years, when we couldn't summon the courage to discuss her among ourselves.

Grief, not only of loved ones, but also of anything we hold dear, may cause great personal and mental distress, but it is also the energy when exercised rightly, which produces meaningful and tangible benevolent effects: physically, mentally, spiritually and emotionally; both personally and socially.

I discovered this reality from an almost forced memory of my mom from childhood, the part of which became integral to my existence. From her empty chair, her birthdays, the anniversaries without her, the many tiny things we missed her for, emotions where we allow time to heal but which we held on to until this busted over the years into words.

Emotions buckled up for so long, at last, became communicable, and once we started talking, we gradually experienced a freedom transcending beyond what was simply personal, but a freedom which was also experienced by our immediate families and well beyond into our societies.

Such experiences, which have become one of my great motivations for writing this book, is one which I shall further explore in the latter chapters of this book also regarding my Dad.

The late Queen Elizabeth II was reputed to observe grief as the price we pay for love, but I can add, purpose is the gift from that grief when we make a proper journey out of it.

I can also identify with the experiences of Princes William and Harry about the pain of loss of their mother. Their devotion towards supporting Mental Health charities must have been informed by the experience of their mental distress at a loss. The toils and the remembrance of her, which in their case was what definitely led to the formation of their characters and has shaped their distinct outlooks and attitudes to life. They have used their grief with positive action to aid their journey back and thus forward.

Creating a Cult out of Memory

Some argue against commemorative practices such as Armed Forces Day, Remembrance Day, Holocaust Memorial Day and D Day to name a few as inconsequential and a waste of time and resources. The experiences through the remembrance of my mom show how developing activities around the loss of her were psychologically beneficial to my own and my family's well-being. I would argue that community or national experiences, where we collectively remember, help personal, national and international healing and well-being.

Regarding my mom, unlike national remembrances we did not do anything grand, we acknowledged her birthdays and her death day. We contributed to make a memorial on her graveyard. We still go to her graveside every year to say a short prayer. Not forgetting her was the principal act we embarked on together, and this was eventually rewarding.

These simple rituals (which could easily be disregarded and not actioned) are what developed an awareness in me of how potent the active memory of loved ones can help to bear the pain of loss whilst growing up mentally, spiritually and emotionally.

We tend to worry about the fate of our departed loved ones. The story of their welfare after death, if we search deep enough is really not so much about them, but about us! We can learn a lot about this from the proper utilisation of memory.

Lest We Forget

When death strikes there are two victims: the one who departs and the survivor who goes through the rabbit hole of grief because of their love. Coming out safely at the other end depends on the right attitude.

As with my mom, from the period when our loss rang through our heads individually, to the times when we were able to speak about it, through to the significant moments of our lives (graduating from college, getting married, having babies) her memory played a decisive role.

For instance, my brother and I, upon having our first girls shared between us her names, I chose her first name, Mercy, and he chose her second name, Titilayo, for our daughters.

Her memory has also informed our involvements in our families and the charities we either have supported or which we have set up in Africa.

It is a gift that cannot be bought, you earn it by living it, or else it becomes ephemeral. Most purposeful charities which benefit

Principle 6: COHERENCE – Memory is the Vehicle out of Chaos

society are borne of such experiences propelled by grief. This is what I call purpose.

Goodwill is not enough to understand the 'aliveness of memory'. An openness and depth to our human experience is necessary. In order to judge the reality of memory sufficient affection will be required. It is this which would allow us to appreciate, to know, to give, and to do.

Whenever you are beaten and downtrodden, exercise memory. Memory of what you may ask? Look back and ask:

- ◉ How did those in your situation make it up?
- ◉ What brought about the happy moments you initially enjoyed? and
- ◉ What could you have done better?

Many underestimate the shear energy to be derived from a simple art of listening to memory.

Using Memory Patterns

The philosopher Søren Kierkegaard wrote, *"Life can only be understood backward; but it must be lived forwards."*

In order to live this moment in a positive way, we must focus on our future (vision) whilst utilising the past (memory) to sustain the vision.

Anyone who fails to learn from history is destined to repeat it. If we are to live the present well and to prepare for a benevolent future in both our public and private lives, we must exercise memory, for history does live in the present.

The past moves and does not happen exactly the same, this is why in this age of intense disruptions we should not succumb to the temptation of repeating 'good old days'. Remember, no two days are the same!

Memory allows us to see patterns because what has happened before will happen again, and what has been done before will be done again, but not necessarily in the same manner. We need to extrapolate what was positive and discard the negative, thus changing the 'good old days' to 'good learnt actions' which are recycled from the past. A meaningful journey is not about forgetting the past, rather it is about incorporating this past in the right manner to enable one to:

- Move forward into the future.
- Develop a mindset which can find meaning from chaos.
- Heal our holistic selves to purify remembrance and not forget.

We can do this as a society by

- Including history, biography, and autobiography of success into our curriculum.
- Developing a reading and writing culture in schools, families, and communities.

Ultimately, it is about valuing whatever legacy has been left for posterity.

The discipline to develop is not to take things for granted. It is imperative to look forward while gaining strength from memory because without learning from the past, it is difficult to craft a future.

Memory's Purpose to our Reality

One purpose of memory is to extract what is real and to recover lessons through a reiterating action and shared experiences which bolster our impression of what to do and how to do it, how to act and how not to act.

Practices such as the days of Remembrance should not be seen simply as practices borne out of traditional norms, but

Principle 6: COHERENCE – Memory is the Vehicle out of Chaos

fundamentally they have utility and serve as powerful means of healing and purifying the past.

The past needs to be addressed and confronted, not forgotten. Problems can arise when people are told to 'forget' because, through the past, we can discern patterns and gain insight into positive trends which we can be maximized and discover risks to disregard or avoid.

Sometimes, from a misguided idiom we may be asked to *'forgive and forget'*, I reiterate we must remember not to forget. It is impossible to simply *'forget'*, when what we need is to remember which aids our healing, otherwise the hurt rears its ugly head.

History has an energy to be cultured and properly nurtured, as Winston Churchill said, *"The farther backward one can look, the farther forward one would see."*

When we take out time to reflect, we can understand events surrounding us and can better utilise memory to solder together historical and cosmic processes scattered across time.

Present realities can be formed by memory, and memory itself is strong to the extent that we can personify events and processes in such a way that they become, not just a remembrance but a potent energy with a unique utility of its own.

Poor Use of Memory

Collective memory is beneficial for any society as it is from here that culture develops. Disenfranchising collective memory results in staleness and produces an apathy of society, and as a result, there is little or no progress.

In our age, we have wallowed in apathy and have removed long-used memory by not paying attention to what DOES need to be sustained.

For instance, because of the unfair experiences of the past, some have tapped into past angers to breed the present religious, racial, economic, environmental and political divides and have in the process 'thrown away the baby with the bath water'.

Justice is needed, but we should not lurk in the past such that we fail to live in the present. In a true healing process, a natural forgetfulness will occur to the negative experiences of the past and we move on to living the present which consists in battling against current human miseries of our age, such as inequality, ignorance, hunger, mediocrity and sickness, but without anger and resentment.

On the other hand, perpetuating the causes of our 'hero's past' with the same strategies and methods which were only relevant in their cultural times, without any creative application to the current times, will expose us more to the domain of the Journey Back, until we have learned the lessons. Ordeal forces wisdom and eventually propels mission without abandoning memory.

Memory is the guide between Journey Back and Journey Forward. We need to be able to balance the utility of the past with a forward-looking mentality to build something sustainable for ourselves and society.

A pearl of African wisdom says, *'When a young person falls, he looks forward, but when an adult falls, he looks backward.'*

Young people have dreams and drive, because of their ambition, even if they are beaten or fail, they have the tendency to be more forward-looking toward their future potential. Responsible adults who are fallen, often look back through an assessment of their lives by considering what they have done in the past for them to believe they deserve their current state.

Principle 6: COHERENCE – Memory is the Vehicle out of Chaos

Memory utilised through a combination of these two attitudes and a development of synergy between Tradition and Innovation, helps so much in moving individuals and society foward.

In this case, the old represents the boundary between the past and the present, while the young represents the boundary between the present and the future, inclusivity and diversity must incorporate a synergy of these two.

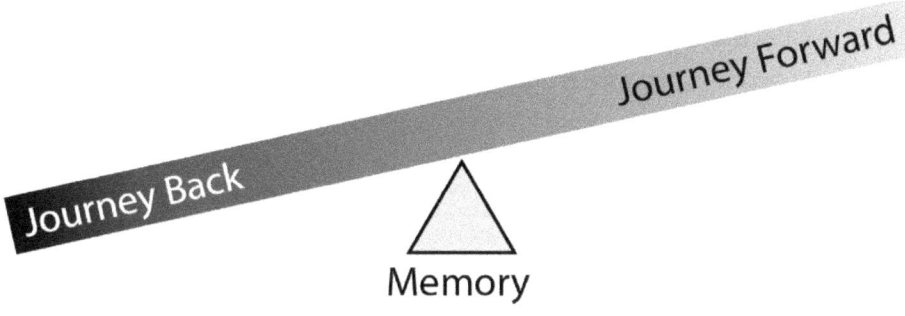

Memory is the Guide between the Journey Back and Journey Forward

In order to live within a liberating moment, we need to have a focus on the future (vision) by utilising the tool of the past (memory).

I shall talk more on the necessity of this balance in a future principle when I discuss why and how leadership should be coordinated for service and peace.

A story told to me by my mom (another cherished memory) impresses more on me (in adulthood) a contemporary meaning of an African folktale. It is about how the dog was rescued by her mother. It goes like this:

Blooming Through Chaotic Times

An Alujonjonkijon Fable

There was a famine in the animal kingdom. This famine had lasted so long that any existing source of food had been completely depleted.

The animals knew they had to do something or they would all die one by one. They called a meeting where every animal was in attendance. It was agreed that each would have to sacrifice and eat his mother to ensure the continuation of the animal species.

The dog who had been at the meeting decided to the contrary. He secretly resolved he was not going to sacrifice his mother, so he hid her in the sky.

Every day, he would secretly go to a particular spot where he sang a song asking his mother to drop a rope and the dog

The Dog with his Mother in the Sky

would climb to the sky where his mother would have a feast waiting for him.

He always eats to his satisfaction while the other animals continued to be affected by famine, even after eating their mothers.

The meaning behind the Alujonjokijon Tale

Each animal's acquiescence to kill its mother, is an indirect decision to halt their potential. In normal language, we can say, just like the other animals, the dog also lost his mum. But to 'eat' means to discard, because you dispose , or excrete what is eaten.

But 'taken to the sky' as the dog has done, means not forgetting. Memory, deep enough, brings back the dead to life. The real misfortune is forgetfulness and neglect.

The other animals, out of the consequence of famine in the land had been driven towards a temporary solution, but the dog had thought deeper and instead resolved in a sense, to keep the memory of his mom alive and sustain the narrative, albeit modified.

Memory is a necessary tool not only for navigating turbulent periods which tend to stop us or deter us in making progress, but a major tool for freedom.

When the dog's mother was in the sky and not with him, he kept her memory alive by simple rituals which connected him to her and allowed him to be sustained, even while the other animals still wallowed in suffering after eating their moms.

I shall tell the concluding part of this story in the next Principle, where I shall discuss how memory bears a great significance, especially when tied to motherhood. We shall see how, we can be in danger of annihilating memory without the regard for motherhood; and if we do this, we have little chance of blooming forward from the Journey Back.

Practical Suggestions for Memory

1. Actively think of a departed loved one you miss, write down any poignant memories which guide you.
2. Actively think about a significant event which has shaped you, note how you have been positively changed by it.
3. Create a personal or group practice of healing through remembrance.

PRINCIPLE 7. COHERENCE - BLOOM THROUGH THE PATH OF MOTHERHOOD

Motherhood is the domain of our education and livelihood.

Francis Niyi Akinola

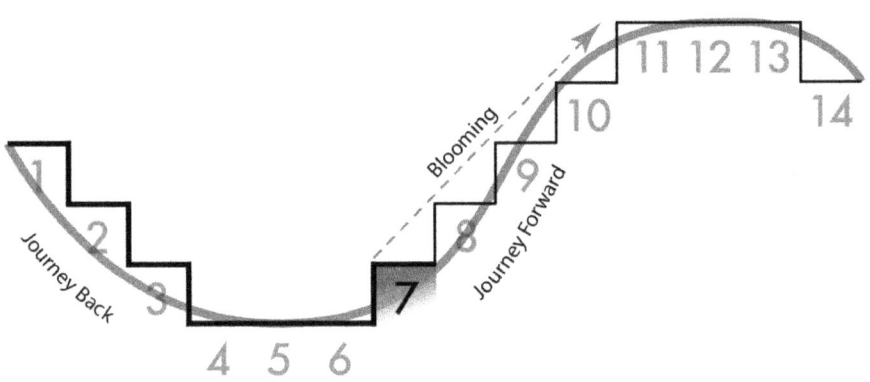

Principle 7

Principle 7: COHERENCE – Bloom Through the Path of Motherhood

We can proceed to the Journey Forward through birth by the mother. Here, I would like to consider this birth in the context of three dimensions of motherhood:

1. The first is the land of our birth or adoption which I term as Nature.
2. The second is our Biological Mothers, which I term as Nurture.
3. The third is the domain of our education, which I term as Alma Mater.

You have travelled this far within the discomforting terrain and struggle of the Journey Back and now as you arrive at the tipping point of your liberation, it is necessary that you do not let go of the entity which will foster thriving: Motherhood.

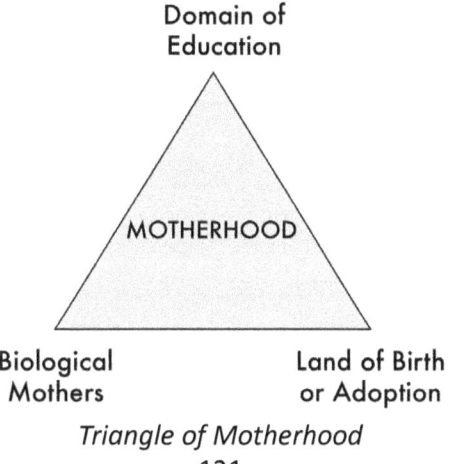

Triangle of Motherhood

Motherhood is the bedrock of every culture, it provides a shield in crisis and ultimately produces life. As such it deserves our care and reverence.

Mothers work so that their children can thrive. Children, in turn, would do well to focus on the well-being of their mother. If this be not the case, the battle is lost from the onset.

Within the three categories of motherhood shown in the previous diagram, it is obvious how a biological mother can be identified as a constituent of motherhood. The two other mothers, the Alma Mater and the land of birth, are not immediately obvious, but they bear similar importance towards our thriving.

These dimensions of motherhood are next to sacred, as they constitute the core of our labour and we should realise how they serve as the means to our rescue and liberation once we take up responsibility for their refinement and reform.

We neither excuse nor destroy these sources of our many toils and sufferings, but reform her. It is easier to take up the responsibility to reform a familiar mother rather than escape into another mater that takes an elongated cycle to master.

1. The Land of Our Birth or Adoption (Nature)

One of the greatest contemporary issues is an ecological one. It is hard to make sense of nature. The increase in greenhouse gases, caused by human activities, including industrial processes, transportation and agriculture, has impacted every living organism's health (including human health) and that of the environment.

Such activities cause global temperatures to rise, leading to sea-level rise, along with air, water and soil pollution. Extreme weather events, other environmental and social impacts, increases in atmospheric carbon dioxide also causes ocean water to become more acidic, causing significant impact on marine ecosystems.

The loss of habitats due to deforestation, pollution, land use change and numerous other factors are causing a decline in the number of species on earth and are leading to a loss of biodiversity, soil degradation and other negative impacts.

Such ecological crises are interconnected and have far-reaching impacts on human societies and the natural world.

Mother Earth

Basic Darwinian theorem states: *'Individuals less suited to the environment are less likely to survive and less likely to reproduce; and individuals more suited to the environment are more likely to survive and thrive at the expense of others.'*

Tyrannical human activity is exploiting the natural world for short-sighted and short-term gain, with little regard for the future. Humans are exemplifying Darwin's maxim stated above. However, I argue that if we do not nurture, respect and protect our natural world, the detriment to the 'weaker' species will ultimately mean us - and create our downfall.

On Care of the Land

The land is important to our survival and over the years, mankind has managed to tame it but often to the detriment of every other species.

Not only has man tamed the land, he has exploited it, using its resources and often neglecting to give back and replenish it. You have a duty of care to the land, both the home you were born to and the land where you choose to live.

In addition to taming the land, mankind has pushed its luck further by exploiting its resources, and in all these, care of the land has been grossly neglected.

There is a saying which goes, *God always forgives, man sometimes forgives, nature never forgives.'* This is not to say nature is wicked, but that nature works on natural laws, one of which says: action and reaction are always equal and opposite.

The survival of the fittest, which is the crux of Darwin's theorem, is becoming increasingly obvious. There is no point advocating for change on a global scale, if we fail to start on the mother care from our 'land', our home, our room.

We all have to bear the responsibility of the care of that domain of our birth or adoption, beginning from the little acts of non-wastage of domestic energy. By simply switching off unused light and heat, nature could reward us for such a consistency. When we do the necessary job of caring for our domain, we thrive. If we do not, we store up the burden of a future chaos and move further down the Journey Back.

On an individual, local and global level, the implementation of renewable and sustainable actions, which can avert or limit crises posed by global warming, is a responsibility which we must take up.

Our environment influences, not just the economy, but also regulates our genetic constituents and thus our survival.

Our survival therefore lies in the nurturing of the land. We must individually attempt to meet the needs of the present without compromising the ability of future generations to meet their need. This is what the term 'environmental sustainability' is all about.

2. Biological Motherhood (Nurture)

The world is in a woman, and its gateway is between her thighs, the energy for running this world comes from her, through Motherhood, it is the case for nurture.

The Unique Mitochondria

An embryo is formed from two sources, the paternal gene from sperm, and the maternal gene from an egg. However, the energy-producing factories of the cell known as mitochondria come exclusively from the female-produced egg.

What this means, in a purely physical and biological sense, is that the survival of the human race and human continuity is the prerogative of women. If women within a domain have only sons, then the mitochondrial lineages will dash against the glass pane of male-only hereditary and vanish in the next generation without any means of producing further offspring.

Motherhood is therefore what makes humans survive because sperm cannot add any mitochondrial genome to their children. All humans, male and female, owe the survival of their species exclusively to the mitochondria produced by their mother. The sperm is only a glorified vehicle for male DNA.

Out of Africa

This mitochondria reality is further explored by scientists through a scientific theory of human evolution known as the 'Out of Africa' or 'Recent African Origin' (as explained in Siddhartha Mukherjee's book 'The Gene: An Intimate Story')

This theory proposes that modern humans (Homo sapiens) originated in Africa and then migrated to other parts of the world, replacing other hominid species such as Neanderthals and Denisovans, suggesting all of humanity can be traced to one single woman from Africa.

This individual is sometimes referred to as, 'Mitochondrial Eve' because genetic studies have shown that all living humans have inherited their mitochondrial DNA (mtDNA) from a single female ancestor who lived in Africa.

According to this theory, the *Most Recent Common Ancestor* (MRCA) of all living humans lived in Africa around 100,000 to 200,000 years ago.

By analysing the mtDNA sequences of different populations around the world, scientists have been able to trace back the ancestry of modern humans to this female ancestor in Africa.

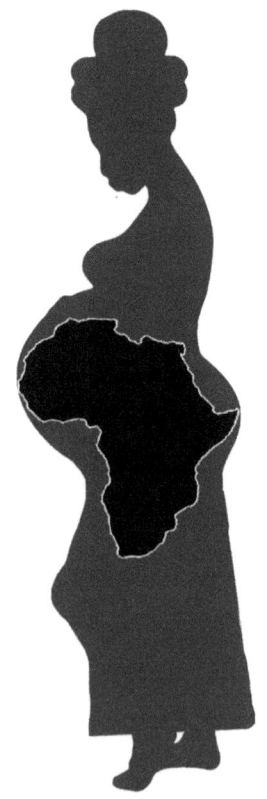

Mother Africa

Principle 7: COHERENCE – Bloom Through the Path of Motherhood

If this theory is correct, based on this analysis on motherhood, we can see an evolutionary confluence between ecology and biology; genetics and memetics; nature and nurture, between 'The land of birth (or adoption) and biological motherhood', and we can say in a sense, all humans have an obligation to 'Mother Africa' as a collegial root, which sadly is one of the most deprived and poverty-stricken regions on earth.

Any domain which births you and helps you to thrive is worthy to be considered sacred. And, even a domain that births you and scars you demands refinement and reform not ridicule and destruction.

An Obligation of Care

As previously stated, the DNA of a woman has a great lot to do with who you are and who you will become. The fate of humanity is entwined with the essence of motherhood and through basic biological laws, there is no escape from any alignment with either a benevolent or any malicious component.

Herein lies the responsibility we owe women. This responsibility is not only about biology, it goes deeper into what it means to be human and thrive.

We have an obligation to threat women kindly, and especially take care of our mothers, for what she becomes in the mind rule, is tied to that which we would be in the future. If we neglect our mothers, we are neglecting our fate in the rule of the mind. If we do not take care of our mothers, we face unpalatable consequences.

What we are now, they were and what they are we shall become. It is a cyclic responsibility. We do a right and justified thing to defend mothers, in life and at death, for what happens to her vibrates into the core of our being and into our eternal destiny.

3. The Domain of Our Education (Alma Mater)

Alma mater takes its etymological root from two Latin words meaning 'nourishing or bountiful mother.' It is an allegorical Latin phrase currently used to identify a school, college, or university that one formerly attended, or graduated from. It can be further projected to be any institution that serves as the source of our knowledge and livelihood and by extension the domain and system where we study, work, and pray.

The term Alma Mater was originally used in Ancient Rome as a way of referring to certain goddesses associated with nourishment, including Ceres and Cybele (Cybele was sometimes also referred to as Magna Mater, meaning "great mother"). Later, the term alma mater was applied to Mary, the mother of Jesus.

Domain of Mind Evolvement

It is no coincidence that this domain of cultured mind evolvement (educational institution) is often referred to as Alma Mater. These institutions of knowledge foster the mental, intellectual, social and spiritual faculties, enabling a person to thrive and as such deserves the term 'mother'.

Institutions of mind evolvement could determine the foundation of what the future of the other two types of motherhood become because knowledge is integral to action.

If we are not taught or have not experienced the previously discussed dimensions as mothers, we may have little motivation or obligation to act at reforming or refining the concept of mother, leaving empty any experience that would attempt to verify their importance.

The sources of our mind evolvement is not limited to educational institutions, they can be any domain where we reorientate our awareness. These can be communities, families, places of worship, of education or cultural institutes

If these sources of mind evolution operate in mediocrity, then the two other mothers (land of birth and natural motherhood) will be subjected to greater manipulation of selfishness, as our minds will be mediocre in their evolution and renewal.

We utilise this motherhood to authentically educate ourselves to freedom because authentic education is the ultimate power, it is the greatest legacy and the portal through which the mother supplies our enablement to bloom!

On the Care of the Biological Mother

How then should devotion to a mother from her children look? Aside material cares which are very important, the mental care of the mother should also be an utmost necessity, for on it depends her future, our destiny and freedom for posterity.

Gently, but firmly, mature children must both learn from and work at the mind renewal of their mothers.

This is a reciprocal activity, for instance, if the mother has only had a material outlook and has not brought up her children on the mental work of renewal, it would be herculean effort for the children to derive the capacity of doing this important work.

When mothers purely raise their children up to focus simply on the ephemeral and material, they are simply digging up their own graves. On a global scale, this is the source of the problem we are experiencing with climate change and global warming.

Change is difficult for a mother but it is on change that our collective blooming depends.

The motherhood categories, of birth, of the land, and of the alma mater, can often be reluctant to change; but everything moves, everything changes, and so, firmly, slowly and gently, we have the task of helping motherhood be the reason for moving and for change. If change is not made, mothers may become like stones; this in turn would create hell because then we all stall.

Back to the Roots

To be free, humanity has to revisit the importance of motherhood in these three areas.

1. To recognize the position of motherhood as the pivotal portal to freedom.
2. To work the mother through an authentic connection to freedom; to be inclusive and value unity over division, even in conflict.
3. To have a passion for the land and value every form of motherhood.

The ideal of motherhood is inclusivity. A thriving mother knows how to unify amidst conflict to expand her bosom. She is always welcoming and uses the synergy of mind evolution to bring about fruitfulness and prosperity of biological motherhood, the land of birth and the cultural domain of mind evolution.

Repairing Motherhood

No one likes their mothers to be messed with. It brings to the fore a primordial instinct of defence, sometimes to a point of irrationality.

But a courageous child, in tune with reality, would want the mother to move if she is in a difficult or non-nurturing scenario, which can leave the mother wondering where to, because, to her, everything is perfect with her.

Children ought to be sympathetic to the complacency mothers may have with the required change because mothers have become accustomed to a certain way of doing things, they may resist. It is important to be gentle but firm and always keep reconciliation as the ultimate focus; try to incorporate their ideas and style into the change. Here I do not only talk about the biological mother but all three variations of motherhood.

I worry when I see how at the slightest provocation, people leave their marriages, their families, their land of birth, or change their communities of worship.

Some decisions create lasting impacts and as such demand more discernment and introspection before embarking on them. Only by careful considerations may life changing motherhood escapes be made.

If the mother has not harnessed and valued the process of positive change throughout the growth of their children, the children themselves will not necessarily value change and continued rebirth.

Without any experiential rebirth children may unwittingly force the mother deeper into mediocrity in the name of change, then stagnancy and poverty could linger long in the household, land or mind.

Motherhood requires care and nurture. When motherhood becomes stale and does not follow the path of authenticity, it spirals back into the journey back, which the concluding part of the Alujonjonkijon fable, the dog and his mother, started in Principle 6 illustrates well.

An Alujonjonkijon Folktale: Concluding Tale

The African folktale tells of the dog, who during famine in the animal kingdom, and in a bid to perpetuate livelihood for himself hid his mother in the sky rather than to sacrifice her as required by the animal kingdom consensus.

The dog hid his mother in the sky instead of sacrificing her, and he would sing to her from a particular spot, then climb a rope, lowered by his mother to join her for a feast.

He continued this practice until one day, as the dog was singing for his mother to drop the rope, the tortoise (who is always the cunning trickster in African folktale) was passing by. He hid himself to observe what was going on. He heard the song the dog sang, saw the rope being dropped from the sky and the dog climb up it.

The following day, the tortoise went to the same spot and disguising his voice, he sang the song he had heard the dog sing the day before. A rope dropped from the sky and the tortoise began to climb this rope. At this same time, the dog was just approaching the same spot and he saw the tortoise climbing to the sky.

The dog immediately started to sing to his mother. This time, he sang that he was not the one climbing the rope and his mother should cut the rope. The dog's mother got a pair of scissors and cut the rope sending the tortoise crashing to the ground.

This caused the Tortoise's shell to break into several pieces. He managed to glue these pieces together but that is how the tortoise ended up with the rough shell we know today.

Morals of the Concluding Story

The moral of the story is firstly, if you haven't got a first-hand vision or knowledge of motherhood, it is difficult to replicate the benefit. This is what the tortoise was attempting which led to his shell being broken.

There is an experience which may be personal or may be acquired from the institute of the 3rd Motherhood, the Alma Mater.

Principle 7: COHERENCE – Bloom Through the Path of Motherhood

Mother Dog throwing the rope to her 'son'

Secondly, everyone's experience is unique and if you are not patient with the benefits Motherhood (as the other animals demonstrated by eating their mothers) and you practice apathy or abscondment, taking a short-cut towards reaping the benefits, may end catastrophically. The path to liberation through motherhood demands patience within the realm of time and space and you cannot take a short cut. We must patiently draw from yesterday's lessons and make use of priority judgements which help us to thrive more easily than when one does not.

Thirdly, Motherhood can be nurturing yet fearsome. The mother will use her experience and maturity to use both these facets of her nature. She understands both must be integrated into the holistic experience of life, which is ultimately moving forward, despite its back-and-forth motion (my initial description of life's experience).

Motherhood itself is a forward-moving entity, but without the right utilisation of her, one may, like the tortoise work towards crashing one's back. The real flaw arises out of cutting corners for freedom. This is the same for our biological mothers, the land of our birth or adoption and the space for our mind evolvement.

I'd like to finish my thoughts on Motherhood with the words expressed in Anthem from the musical Chess. It is a beautiful tribute to Motherhood as the land of birth

Words from Anthem

How can I leave her?
Where would I start?
Let man's petty nations tear themselves apart
My land's only borders lie around my heart

Practical Suggestions for Motherhood

1. Share a thought for your biological mother (alive or dead). When last did you make an act of gratitude to her?
2. Share a thought for the land. What have you proactively done for the environment in your life.
3. Which institutions have created the greatest impact on you? What are you doing to sustain the connection with them?

Principle 7: COHERENCE – Bloom Through the Path of Motherhood

Blooming Through Chaotic Times

PART TWO
THE JOURNEY FORWARD

Achieving a breakthrough brings a sense of empowerment and confidence and demonstrates that one is capable of overcoming challenges and achieving goals, and leads to a greater sense of self-belief and self-assuredness.

Achievement of an objective can be as simple as passing an examination, getting a promotion, or getting married, or it can be as lofty as the discovery of penicillin, the invention of the telephone, the development of the internet, the mapping of the human genome, or the discovery of the Theory of Relativity, and, as Albert Einstein himself puts it upon the discovery of Relativity:

"The years of searching in the dark for a truth that one feels but cannot express, the intense desire and the alternations of confidence and misgiving until one breaks through to clarity and understanding, are known only to him who has experienced them himself."

These years described above are ones of toil and hardship where the Journey Back had won which now needs to be preserved during the Journey Forward.

You have attained a unique phase where you can exercise freedom. You have now become a System, the Establishment. Now, you have a unique opportunity to correct and live right those aspects which once disgusted you and which you have in the past criticized.

But remember, you are, yourself in a criticism section, because, this freedom bequeaths on you the responsibility to judge structures and design processes as an integral aspect of the System; and you better act right, because you are under scrutiny.

Now you are free. But there is something beyond freedom: work, love, belief and a commitment to something. Freedom is not enough. It is what you do with freedom - what you give it up for, in service of others which matters!

The Journey Forward happens as a positive experience in line with the premise of this book regarding life as a forward and expansive movement. Having thrived amidst the chaos of the Journey Back, your duty now is to keep the 'big picture in perspective. To build on the victories achieved and to keep safe the freedom attained.

By transcending through the Journey Back into the Journey Forward we achieve a sense of purpose, which is the primal freedom, and, this sense of freedom, as Isaiah Berlin relates, *"is freedom from chains, from imprisonment, from enslavement by others."* The rest - according to Berlin - *"is extension of this sense, or else metaphor."*

The Journey Forward experience is about building authentic and lasting confidence which produces freedom, develops influence and builds a lasting legacy. The Journey Forward is not only about learning, but it is the path thread by protagonists who impact societies, mould cultures and impact our world!

BLOOMING

The Blooming Principles

These Principles explore the ways and attitudes whereby our newfound victory can be sustained unto further successes.

PRINCIPLE 8. BLOOMING - PRACTICE GRATITUDE

Life's fuel is gratitude.

Francis Niyi Akinola

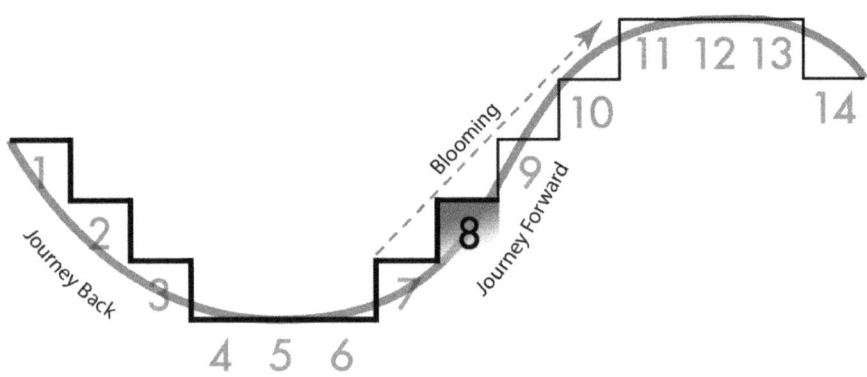

Principle 8

Principle 8: BLOOMING – Practice Gratitude

The feelings one experiences after achieving freedom and a breakthrough are relief, joy, and excitement. It is as though a heavy burden has been lifted off one's shoulders. The sheer peace experienced by one's efforts having paid off introduces a new paradigm to existence.

How does one give momentum to sustain a sudden experience of breakthrough? It is through an attitude of gratitude proceeding from the heart but translating into action.

After achieving a breakthrough, it is common to feel grateful for the support and resources which helped make it possible. This may include gratitude towards friends, family, colleagues and mentors who provided guidance and encouragement.

However, it is harder to continue a practice of gratitude as a life attitude. After the thrill of the initial breakthrough, mankind tends to forget how they have attained that state in the first instance.

An African adage says, '*It is a fool who forgets an act of authentic goodness done to him.*' It is important to be grateful, for this gives us sustenance. Without working to discover more reasons in our lives for which to show gratitude, we shall stall and fade away.

Developing Gratitude as a Lifetime Mindset

From Principle 7 : Bloom Through the Path of Motherhood, I argued on how cooperation with motherhood, births and initiates a final escape from the Journey Back, but what catches this freedom and propels one's experience into the Journey Forward is gratitude. The Journey Forward requires gratitude as an energy before it can move and be sustained. Gratitude is the fuel of this part of the experience.

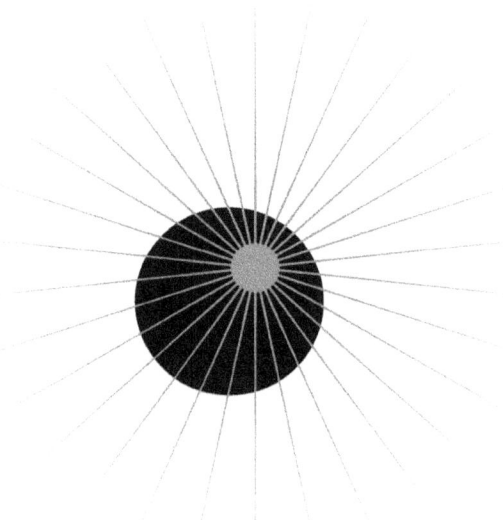

Burst of Gratitude

The reason to be grateful means something has happened to us which creates an improvement from our past situation. When we use gratitude as a tool, we can feel something is already happening. We are now caught up in the energy of the future.

The Future is Here

The future is about the Journey Forward and gratitude fuels that future. It supplies the power for hope and optimism. Developing and sustaining an attitude of gratitude produces a multiplicity of freedom, where we can self-actualise ourselves.

Principle 8: BLOOMING – Practice Gratitude

When we thank anyone about anything, we are raising the moral pedestal of such a person. When we affirm a person, we also show them our positive values. The practice of gratitude can take many forms, but its psychological effect enables us to experience reality through a positive dimension, which enhances our liberation. The more we capitalise on gratitude, the more we expand on freedom, wealth and surpluses even of mind, heart and spirit.

The entire fabric of the Journey Forward should be lit by a heart of gratitude as it is a powerful energy to be utilised in order for a person to experience the realm of freedom.

What is There to be Grateful About ?

In life, where the force of a single calamity can overwhelm many a victorious event, one may wonder what there is to be grateful about.

We are genetically wired towards focusing on the one thing which needs to be resolved in our lives and we often lose sight of the many things which have been overcome.

The overwhelming nature of life gravitates us towards thoughts of the many unresolved problems beleaguering us and we seem to align ourselves toward complaint rather than gratitude. We all have things we are looking forward to achieving and it takes work and discipline to think towards gratitude.

Do not take the present serenity you may feel for granted. You enjoy it because some people have laboured to achieve this serenity for you. Fate has worked to get you here despite the common, widespread elements of chaos (death, disease, and destruction) surrounding us. You have been lucky to be alive from the onset, for, out of a million sperm cells, one stuck with your mother's ovum to make you. You have continued to beat the odds of survival to this point.

You, a stardust from nowhere, have survived within an ecosystem of Darwinian struggle and have (through an environment which thrives on 'survival of the fittest', where the weakest become the prey of the dominant powers) bloomed!

You beat the odds, and you have not simply survived but, despite weakness and frailty, have thrived through that survival and are still taking your chances at progress.

Be grateful, and use this gratitude to boost your chances of survival. If you stop being grateful, only a breath of chaos may lie in wait to negate your chances of continued survival and success. Complaints and negativity sure do increase chaos' chances.

Thank your parents, your mentors, your society, and whoever has given you the opportunity for this benevolence; action this emotion of gratitude to also lift those struggling from the cycle of the Journey Back out from their blues.

There are so many forces which conspire against progress and as progress can be quiet and unassuming it may pass by unnoticed. It is thus necessary to look for ways to continually search for the positivity of gratitude in order to ensure health, wealth, happiness and success; but it takes work and discipline to think towards gratitude.

If one loses out on gratitude, one becomes discontent or sad and could spiral back into the Journey Back, where the exercise of the work involved produces greater stress due to limited freedom. You may undo all the hard work you have already put into the process. The challenge is how to make a positive, grateful heart sustainable in the midst of all the discouragement and discomfort.

Optimism Fuels Gratitude

Optimism is a predetermined mindset. It ought to be practised regardless of the negative circumstances surrounding us which combat against a heart of gratitude. But, realistically and practically, mankind really does have a lot to look forward to and be grateful for.

Books such as *Factfulness* by Hans Rosling and *The Better Angels of our Nature* by Steven Pinker reveal how we can be wired against the progress made by humanity across the ages but especially in the 20th and 21st century. We focus on the negative news that proliferates the media and thereby lose sight of reasons to be grateful and optimistic.

In *Factfulness,* Rosling through scientific data, shows how global poverty, child mortality and natural disasters have drastically reduced, and how income level, women's education, individual lifespan have improved.

He also shows, despite this empirical evidence how our negative impulses such as fear lead us to think things have drastically regressed.

I write as an African who is confronted daily by real events and situations which give reason for despair and makes one want to lose faith in the positivity and progress of life. Some may wonder how I can talk about optimism in the face of the realities of existential threats such as global warming, nuclear weapons, economic downturn, and energy crisis, to name a few.

Optimism is not Opposed to Realism

Yet I know, from practice, science and experience that progress and optimism eventually win and it is reasonable to bet and stake our lives on this. Optimism, in my conviction is one reason I wrote this book.

Realistic positivism and progress are not difficult to arrive at for an aspiring person once we master gratitude.

My Positive Reality

I try to live an optimistic life irrespective of what I go through. From an obscure hinterland of Nigeria, and losing my mom at ten years old, I discovered, from experiencing many failures that happiness and wealth is not extrinsic but intrinsic. Though, intrinsic happiness sure does win many positive extrinsic experiences, too.

I am grateful for a stable family environment, both nuclear and extended, which helped solidify my positive attitude and how simple politeness of saying 'sorry', 'thank you', 'excuse me' and 'please' (we call these STEP) can earn favours from among both peers and strangers.

I give thanks to my teachers from whom I gained a desire to learn, inform and educate myself. To my faith, where I learned the ideal of dependence on a higher Power.

There are many milestones in my life where I have been surrounded by people who have assisted me directly or indirectly in me achieving my purpose.

I am indebted to many, so much so that I continually live in an atmosphere of insufficient gratitude and a little guilt, and ironically, it is this 'pingy' guilt of having not been grateful enough which helps me to multiply my graciousness and sustains my Journey Forward.

Gratitude Has to be Realistic

This emotion of gratitude has to be real and not fabricated. I would not compel anyone to just be grateful without having any reason to be grateful.

Principle 8: BLOOMING – Practice Gratitude

It is far more beneficial for instance, to live authentically through the 'chaos' of 'Stooping to Conquer' or realising our 'woundedness', than living an unrealistic gratitude life despite its enormous benefits.

But the sheer fact of acknowledging that you are at the dawn of the Journey Forward already signifies an escape and liberation from something, no matter how little.

My heart does not naturally gravitate towards gratitude but I am lucky that I never run short of reasons to be grateful or people whom to be grateful for, therefore I do not need to 'fake it'.

If gratitude has to be practical; one may wonder, how do we make it so? The most practicable way is to look back to your memories and show gratitude to people or institutions who have knowingly or unknowingly assisted you in escaping from a circle of bondage.

In Principle 6, I talk of not forgetting, here I reiterate the importance of remembering, remember any good done in your favour, because these acts create opportunities for gratitude, which like breath are meaningful to your persistent survival. I suggest it is also important to remember the wrongs done to us as we can use them in a positive way, to forgive and to learn.

Of course, gratitude can be cultivated. I would offer the following suggestions towards cultivating a heart of gratitude.

Cultivating Gratitude

Cultivating gratitude is a practice that can have numerous benefits, such as increasing happiness, reducing stress, and improving relationships. Here are some ways to cultivate gratitude:

- ◉ Keep a gratitude journal: Write down three things you're grateful for each day. This will help you focus on the positive aspects of your life.

- ◎ Practice mindfulness: Pay attention to the present moment and be grateful for what you have in that moment. I shall discuss this in detail in the next chapter.
- ◎ Express your gratitude: Make effort to break the ice and verbally say thank you to someone who has helped you or made a positive impact on your life.
- ◎ Practice positive self-talk: Instead of focusing on what you don't have, focus on what you do have and express gratitude for it.
- ◎ Volunteer: Giving back to others can help you appreciate what you have and feel grateful for the opportunity to help others.
- ◎ Focus on the positive: Try to reframe negative situations in a positive light and focus on what you learned from the experience.

Remember, cultivating gratitude is a practice which takes time and effort. Start small, be consistent and gradually increase the amount of time you spend focusing on the positive aspects of your life.

How you think and feel creates your state of being, thus mastering a mindset of gratitude is a powerful and efficacious way towards making progress and maintaining victory; it is also mentally rewarding because, as we get hold of these reasons, however small, we look forward in hope and find reasons for progress.

Gratitude is an Unforced Act: The P & Ps

Gratitude ought not to be made at the cost of mortgaging our conscience, because we also have to be realistic about tyrannical domains who would seek to force out our generosities. I call such entities P & P, meaning Power and Principalities.

Principle 8: BLOOMING – Practice Gratitude

More often than not, such entities have a stake to your progress, directly or indirectly, as such they act through the System to demand their 'rights', even at the detriment of your 'stability'.

We find these P & Ps rife in history and in our times but under different guises in families, communities and societies.

Some Historical Examples of P & Ps

The forces attempting to gain gratitude from others are numerous throughout history and many of them have an inhumane nature.

During the colonial era, European powers often forced native peoples to express gratitude for their 'civilising' efforts, which included forced conversion to Christianity, destruction of indigenous cultures and economic exploitation.

Slave owners often expected gratitude from their slaves for providing food, clothing, and shelter, despite the fact they were being forced to work without pay and subjected to inhumane treatment.

During the feudal era, lords expected gratitude from their vassals for providing protection and support. However, this gratitude was often coerced, as vassals were required to pledge

Overpowering P & P

loyalty to their lord and provide military service in exchange for land and protection.

Throughout history, men have often expected gratitude from women for their protection and support, despite the fact that women were often marginalized and oppressed. This expectation of gratitude was a way for men to maintain their power over women and justify their unequal treatment.

It's important to recognize that forcing gratitude from others is not an effective way to cultivate genuine appreciation and can often be harmful. Instead, gratitude should be freely given and received, without coercion or expectation.

Dealing Under P & Ps

A Yoruba adage, states, 'eni t'o ju ni lo le ju ni nu' , that is , *"The more powerful person has the potential to gain an undue right of an inferior."* Power can be very ruthless to the weak, and we find this circumstance rife in the ecosystem of mankind.

The System is necessary, and unfortunately P & Ps exist within it. It is necessary to deal wisely with these powers or they can easily force you into a Journey Back. When we experience and are overpowered by such P & Ps, we should try to negate the person's actions by not being confrontational because of the stake they have in our achievements; and because there still looms the potential of spiralling into the Journey Back if they decide to strike hard back at you.

The method of work required in this case should be more psychological than physical. It might be prudent for you to review Principle 2: Stoop to Conquer but Look Up if this happens.

Principle 8: BLOOMING – Practice Gratitude

Acknowledging the Non-P & Ps in the System

It is our responsibility towards progress to continually acknowledge those who have not sought rewards, those who may not even be aware that they have played an integral role in our freedom.

These people are worth finding and it is to our advantage to be gracious if we are to sustain our freedom. Look into the past and show gratitude to those who have been of assistance to you.

The energy of gratitude is abundant but it needs to be worked on using exercises of critical and deep thinking irrespective of our life circumstances.

We ought not to take any act for granted. The mark of a deep and clear thinker is manifested in a gracious spirit. Think, be gracious, and thrive. There is an abundance of reward in gratitude.

We have to take proactive steps towards digging for authentic reasons to be grateful. Always search for reasons to be gracious and look into those people who have been of help and say thank you, either through service, calls, or affirmations.

The Consequences of Gratitude

There is a concept I like amongst the Yoruba people. It is called 'Yiniyini'. This describes the process of 'affirming someone'. The full explanation of 'Yiniyini' is 'Yiniyini k'eni o se mi'. This means when you 'affirm' someone, such person would look altruistically towards you and in return is likely to want to assist you more. It is one of the laws of the universe. It breeds reciprocity. It's a simple 'Givers gain®' mantra which I learnt from Dr Ivan Misner. When one is grateful, he gets more and those who are most successful are the most adept at this act of gratitude.

Gratitude has a multiplying effect. Progress can be sustained only through this. We need not take anything for granted and not lose people before we know their worth.

Seek out people who have helped you. Thank them with sincerity and state how their help has affected you: be specific. Practise gratitude of the mind and in action: use the list of actions in 'Cultivating Gratitude' on pages 149-150 to assist you in this.

Being Proactive with Gratitude

Since gratitude has to be manifested in action, another way of practicing gratitude is to acknowledge your luck at escaping from the Journey Back. It is also necessary to make these acts of gratitude, not simply an individual affair but a communal, national or even a global one.

I have often been intrigued with the United States Thanksgiving holidays celebrated since 1789, a custom worthy of emulation, where families come together to be grateful for blessings received and where people make peace. This is also acted out by the significance of a fun tradition of the President of the United States 'pardoning a turkey' every year.

Finally, Realistic Thinking

I have argued that it is gratitude which fuels the Journey Forward, but something thus fuels gratitude itself. This is clear, deep, and realistic thinking.

We have to practice this, otherwise, we shall forget, and when we forget, we shall cease being gracious.

We can only preserve memory through the practices which I shall describe in the Principle 9:Mindfulness and Meditation.

Principle 8: BLOOMING – Practice Gratitude

Practical Suggestions for Practising Gratitude

1. Think of five things you are grateful for.
2. Say affirmations 'I am grateful for ...' for 10 minutes.
3. Repeat Steps 1 and 2 on a daily basis. Make note of everything you say. See what happens after a month. Please share your findings and thoughts with me. I would love to hear how these practises help you.

PRINCIPLE 9. BLOOMING - SUSTAIN FOCUS

Eternal vigilance is the price of freedom.

Thomas Jefferson

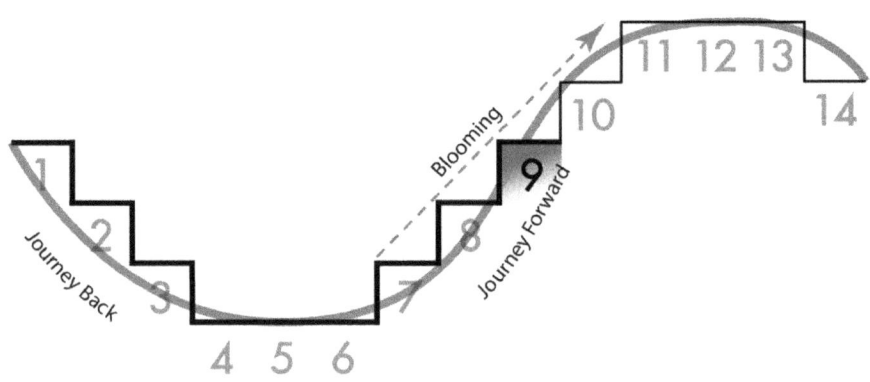

Principle 9

Principle 9: BLOOMING – Sustain Focus

A truly gracious mind is optimistic about the future because, in a way, he has already begun to live the future. In order to sustain this bright future, a grateful person ought to keep and sustain focus by engaging in mindfulness and meditation which is best employed in solitude and silence.

Mindfulness is necessary to call us back to ourselves. Meditation is useful for us to reflect, from self and beyond self.

It is proper to employ solitude because we live in a culture which has a dread of being alone and is always longing to connect. Silence is necessary because we are in an ecosystem of noise which does little to aid mental well-being.

Solitude is sometimes referred to as, 'the Luxury of the Wealthy'. This is because the modern cultural system often constantly engages us. It requires a level of freedom to 'buy' oneself off from the noise.

It is through solitude and silence that we are able to meditate and mindfully perceive and exercise sensation, thought, and imagination. It is from here that our ideas and creativity are formed.

Principle 9 leads us to discuss the reason why someone living the freedom of the Journey Forward must do so with careful and mindful focus and perception on themselves and the circumstances surrounding them.

Empowerment without vision and direction is anarchy. This Principle discusses the process of refining vision and having a clear direction.

What is Mindfulness?

Mindfulness is a mental state which is achieved by focusing one's awareness on the present moment, while calmly acknowledging and accepting our feelings, thoughts, and bodily sensations.

Through an exercise of our mental faculties, we enter a space of self-reflection and place ourselves in a healthy mental state, relaxing and calming ourselves.

As mentioned before, it is said, *'If the eye stays calm, it shall see the nose.'* There are many 'knows', which can be discovered through mindfulness and meditation.

Mindfulness is unique to the individual and the successful implementation and integration of these practices will enable us to focus and to Journey Forward.

When mindfulness is properly practiced, you may see what to do and acquire the power to do it but, as per the practice, there is no one method or technique to achieving the result of mindfulness.

Mindfulness

Principle 9: BLOOMING – Sustain Focus

The Private Dimension of Mindfulness

The uniquely private and personal dimension of this practice does not mean it cannot be learnt, but the onus of this experience cannot be directly imparted by the teacher.

The experience of mindfulness and meditation in solitude and silence is a deeply personal one but one which can translate into a collective focus and action in order to sustain a System.

The starting point of mindfulness for every individual, family, community, organization or institution is self-observation, self-knowledge and self-awareness. From here we can begin to review the lessons from our experience and see how everything is interlinked and how our individual actions can contribute to collective progress.

Only the contemplative mind can bring forward the new consciousness needed to awaken a more loving, just, and sustainable world, including the wisdom and practices to support transformation and inspire loving action.

Why Focus?

When we are successful, there are many distractions that will surface. We have to maintain a focus on building upon success, or what we hold dear will crumble. Mindfulness and meditation will enable us to focus on and identify what is needful and essential.

In modern society we are full of options and choices, and everything beckons on our attention so much that it is more difficult to make choices on the needful and necessary without distractions.

Winston Churchill once said, *"To look is one thing, to see what you look at is another. To understand what you see is another. To learn from what you understand is something else. And to act on what you learn is all that really matters!"*

Decision-making and judgment calls are not always straightforward. For instance, I once was in a conversation with a professional associate about the short span of most employees within organisations. He stated, 'This is because we follow after the money'. How true this is in the entire corporate world. Numerous studies have shown that money is the primary reason why people quit jobs for better opportunities.

It can be difficult to know what the long-term effect of such decisions is on an individual level. It is the nature of the age we are in, but I can see daily how short-term financial decisions act like gravity impacting the long-term direction of many and can result in a massive case of future crisis.

Life's decisions made solely on economic terms can pull one off the beam of one's vision, and once vision is lost, focus decays and we become blind or distracted not knowing where to exist.

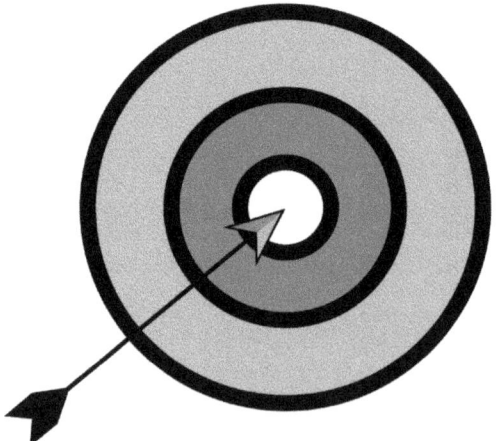

The Arrow Focuses on the Target

Principle 9: BLOOMING – Sustain Focus

The Fisherman and the Businessman

Once, a businessman visited a small fishing village and saw a fisherman coming back from the sea with a large catch.

The businessman congratulates the fisherman on his successful catch and asks him how long it took him to catch so many fish.

The fisherman replies that it only took him a few hours. The businessman suggested the fisherman could spend more time fishing and catch even more fish, which would allow him to make more money and eventually buy a larger boat.

"With a larger boat", he admonished the fisherman, "you could catch even more fish and eventually hire other fishermen to work for you."

"What would you do with all the extra money?" the fisherman asked the businessman.

"Getting such money, I could retire early and spend my remaining days fishing, traveling, and enjoying life", the businessman responded.

"But isn't that what I'm already doing!" The fisherman then retorted.

The Moral of the Story

The story is meant to illustrate the importance of mindfulness and living in the present moment.

The fisherman enjoys the simple pleasures of fishing and spending time with his family, and he is grateful for what he has. In contrast, the businessman is focused on the future and the idea of accumulating more wealth and possessions. He is not fully present in the moment and does not appreciate the simple pleasures of life the fisherman enjoys.

A discovery of ourselves can perpetuate our progression and enable us to be the best version of ourselves.

Don't Act in Haste

I remember when I was in employment how certain colleagues would complain about their circumstances, leave a job for another, and still complain about what they've got and wanting to return to their previous job.

I do not suggest searching for greener pastures is right or wrong but the perception of a better place without evidence clouds our judgement and reduces our ability to make more informed choices.

This also bears relevance to other aspects of our lives. For instance, making life choices with a sole outlook of money can fall short of the happiness and satisfaction one hopes to achieve. Many easily get tired of their current relationship and opt for the next man or woman available, perceived as better or more successful, only to compound their sorrow further when this is not the case. This also applies other tough choices such as the purchase of houses, movement to another country or city, doing business or taking paid jobs, etc.

Many become lured into this spiral and continual cycle of an endless searching for the right choice of life, work and relationships, due to an inability to focus.

When our attention span is shortened, our choices can be shallow due to the nature of a vast number of options. This vast choice can make us endlessly neurotic and impatient. This is where we can lose focus, affecting the depth and significance of our choices and decisions.

The better one is at effective mindfulness practice, the clearer one's judgement becomes. It gives individuals the capability

When Others Can Aid Our Choices

In order to aid our decision-making better, I would propose complementary methods of analysis where other people can better assist us in arriving at better decisions. The implementation of such practices as the Johari's Window, a technique created by psychologists Joseph Luft and Harrington Ingham to help people better understand their relationship with themselves and others will be ideal.

I also learned a very fascinating method similar to but more practical than the Johari Window when reading Hal Elrod's *Miracle Morning*. He proposes we write a letter asking specific friends on specific areas what they have observed in their dealings with us and where they believe we would need to improve. We should be asking friends, whom we know and trust, who would be willing to give us factual advice on how we could mindfully grow.

It takes guts, but this sort of step is beneficial to personal improvement which would aid us better to improve on excellence and to move us up the curve of the Journey Forward. Mindfulness and meditation build in us a strong purpose and meaning which is undeterred by ephemeral lures and immediate desires.

Once purpose is strong enough and the vision is clear, it is possible to not be distracted or dissuaded by the many wiles one encounters along the path.

The Focus of Odysseus

I will return to the narration of Homer's *Odyssey* in this regard. Odysseus was focused on his goals and would not be dissuaded by the many temptations which he encountered.

He was helped by some gods who enhanced his focus and gave him practical advice and means to reach his destination rather than attach himself permanently to the lures and temptations on his journey.

Odysseus was able to develop steadfastness which enhanced his victory and made his home-coming sweet and well-gained.

Leonardo da Vinci once said, *"Once you have tasted flight, you will forever walk the earth with your eyes turned skyward, for there you have been, and there you will always long to return."*

It is worth making the time and effort for solitude and silence and building a routine around mindfulness and meditation in order to sustain focus.

Once we are able to experience their benefits, it becomes difficult to disregard these practices and return to the yoke of the Journey Back.

Eternal Vigilance is the Price of Freedom

Success can sometimes breed complacency when not carefully managed. When you are successful, It is necessary to guard and watch oneself carefully in order not to slip back, and it is in this vigilance over ourselves that we become the best version of ourselves.

We ought to see here, how, it is not activities which need to be expanded but mindfulness. This allows perception and attention to grow, which in turn would enable us to make better decisions through an analysis of different factors, not just upon a dictatorship of money.

Mindfulness is a form of education, and 'Education is growth, it is life itself'. Through education, we continually exercise our intellect, memory, increase our will to learn, plus unlearn and relearn in order to enhance our growth. Education is not simply formal; it is the eternal vigilance to sustain growth. It is the price of the freedom we have achieved!

Solitude and Silence as a Form of Education

The pedagogy of curriculum development in many university systems is quite creative and fascinating.

Usually, the first year is theoretical. You get to know all the brilliant minds in your field and what they have posited regarding your subject of study. You are required to study and know them and write essays about them. The second year is usually devoted to the analysis of prior theories and a critical application of thoughts to their line of thinking. The third year is usually devoted to fieldwork experiences meant to apply and practicalise the theories which have been mastered and to test the analysis we have made.

But, in many higher education institutions, solitude and silence are encouraged but not fostered as a practice and culture integrated into the curriculum. Perception only stops at the level of the intellect at the University.

It is hoped that mindfulness and meditation will develop further in our educational institutions, not just to be another course of study, but as an integrated practice reflecting the fabric of the entire curriculum and as a process required to confront the increasingly complex nature of our culture.

Life is A Balance Between Activities and Stillness

This focused mindfulness and perception, can take many dimensions. Many organizations, for instance, apply a range of technical and statistical analysis to assess and implement decisions.

These methods are right, useful and needed, but they are an insufficient attempt at guarding any freedom attained. Our volatile and complex environment cannot admit only of objective data, we must also implement what I call 'soft practices' such as mindfulness and meditation to achieve and sustain positive momentum.

A singular method based on objective productivity has contributed to the widespread organizational collapse of many businesses. It is estimated by McKinsey that the average lifespan of companies listed in Standard & Poor's (S&P) 500 was 61 years in 1958. Today, it is less than 18 years. Similarly, a study by Innosight found that the average tenure of companies on the S & P's 500 had dropped from 33 years in 1964 to just 24 years in 2016.

These trends suggest that the pace of creativity and innovative technological changes have increased competition, thus making it harder for companies to survive and thrive over the long term.

I believe those who have survived and thrived actively encourage a mindful and reflective culture.

A rediscovery of mindfulness and meditation in order to focus and sustain vision fosters; adaptation, flexibility, and an authentic alignment of values to prevailing changes which, if failed companies had fostered may have continued to survive.

Stillness to Focus is the Journey Forward

It is through the method of silence and stillness where people and organizations can evolve in order to Journey Forward.

More companies have a preference for action and they devote little time and space for solitude, a domain where creative methods are born and where potentials are built.

Principle 9: BLOOMING – Sustain Focus

Enabling processes such as complexity and games theories, business analysis, agile processing, etc. which aids decision making, ought to be complimented by a proactive culture of mindfulness and meditation as an integral process of decision making.

'Soft practices', in the stillness of mindfulness, meditation, is where right perceptions are developed in order to sustain focus on progress. This assists activism towards efficiency.

Devoting Time to Stillness in Organisations

Through stillness, we discover how the silence of our brain gives strength to the entire body. Considerations should be more directed to non-task-oriented processes in a System without which its lifespan would diminish.

For instance, in a typical 8-hour work period, policies can be implemented where an hour should be devoted to 'soft practices' at the workplace.

It may be difficult for decision-makers in our contemporary culture to accept this as not a waste of time. Organisations who implement this as a long-term strategy would benefit from its sustainable effect, as against organisations who are devoted to round-the-clock task processes. Mere activism is not sufficient for success.

Examples of Organisations Practicing Stillness

Google has integrated a mindfulness-based emotional intelligence training program designed to help employees reduce stress and improve well-being. A program which is so popular that it has been adopted by other companies as well.

Apple's 'Mindful Choices' program offers meditation and mindfulness classes to employees. The program is designed to help employees improve their focus, resilience, and emotional intelligence.

General Mills, has a meditation room at its headquarters and offers a 'Mindful Leadership' programme which incorporates mindfulness practices into leadership training and promotes regular mindfulness practices.

Salesforce, a Customer Relationship Management company, practices 'Mindfulness Without Borders', a programme which is designed to help employees reduce stress and improve wellbeing through regular meditation and mindfulness practices.

These are just a few examples of organizations that have recognized the benefits of mindfulness and meditation and have incorporated them into their culture and practices.

By promoting mindfulness and providing resources for employees to reduce stress and improve well-being, these companies are not only improving the lives of their employees but are also creating a more productive and resilient workforce.

Once focus gains momentum, they bring newness and foster creativity, which is the next phase of the Journey Forward and another level of freedom.

Practical Suggestions for Keeping Focus

1. Go to a quiet place, set up an alarm, sit down, close your eyes and do nothing for 10 minutes. After this time, note down any thoughts, feelings or ideas which you experienced during this focus time.
2. Repeat this process the next day but for an extended time period of 20 minutes.
3. Continue to the focus activity for a week. Assess your notings and focus upon any which can be acted upon. Please let me know of your successes.

PRINCIPLE 10. BLOOMING - TINKER ABOUT THE EDGE

We cannot solve a problem with the same thinking we used when we created them.

Albert Einstein

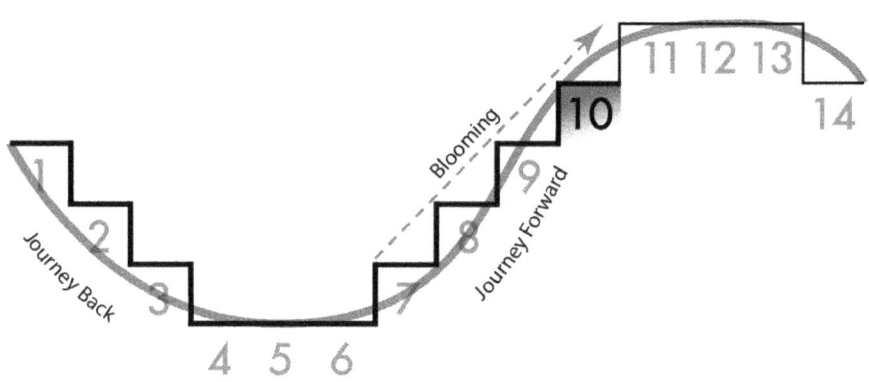

Principle 10

Principle 10: BLOOMING – Tinker about the Edge

Sustaining focus by practicing mindfulness and meditation within a space for solitude and silence are the incubators where ideas can be generated.

We need to try and develop this needful work as a routine. This may be quite challenging in our noisy culture, but it is this aspect of the Journey Forward which is a necessary exercise for reimagination, innovation, and creativity which happens, not at the centre, but along the edge of the histogram (society) and by not following the crowd.

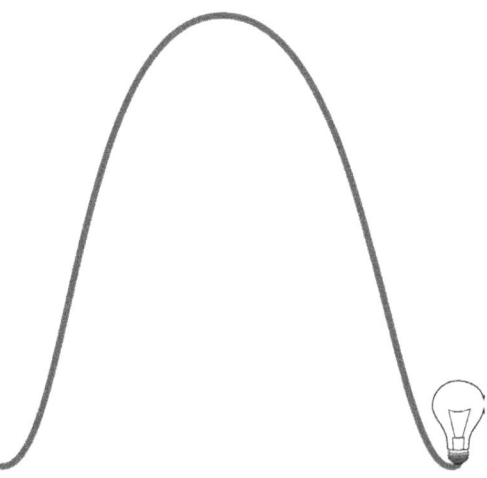

Focus through mindfulness and meditation is a necessary step and the tool for moving forward, that is, living. It is those who would leave their comfort zones, who do *tinker about the edges*, who are interested in living.

Creativity is our Bicycle

Creativity is the vehicle for living. We have to keep moving by finding and developing true but creative ideas, otherwise we shall 'stall and fall' as this simple cyclist story tells:

> As the sun rose over the city, the roads were empty except for one cyclist who was attempting to balance on the spot. He seemed to struggle to maintain his balance, wobbling back and forth on a unicycle.
>
> It was clear he was not a professional circus performer, but he was determined to master this difficult task. He concentrated on his balance, trying to keep his body weight centred and his eyes focused on a fixed point in the distance.
>
> Despite his efforts, the cyclist found it impossible to stay balanced. Every time he got close to achieving it, something would throw him off-kilter and he would have to start again.
>
> Frustrated, he decided to try something different. Instead of trying to stay still, he began to pedal forward, slowly at first, but then with increasing speed. As he moved forward, the cyclist found that maintaining his balance became easier.
>
> He realised he could only maintain balance by moving forward; by pedalling. If he stopped pedalling, he would lose

Principle 10: BLOOMING – Tinker about the Edge

his balance and fall. It was a strange feeling, but one he quickly got used to.

As he rode down the empty streets, the cyclist felt a sense of freedom and exhilaration. He no longer worried, all he had to do was keep moving forward, pedalling one foot after the other.

With a smile on his face, the cyclist continued on his journey, enjoying the simple pleasure of riding his bike and feeling the wind in his hair. He knew there were many challenges ahead, but he was ready for them. As long as he kept moving forward, he would be able to overcome any obstacle that came his way.

Entering this state of continual creativity is what Principle 10 is about, which I term: Tinker about the Edge.

What 'Tinkering' Is

Tinkering involves making small changes to something, especially in an attempt to repair or improve it; and by doing this about the edge, I mean, pushing boundaries, experimenting beyond norms and going beyond our comfort zones.

Albert Einstein says, *"We cannot solve a problem with the same thinking we use in creating them". So,* to make progress we have to undertake the bold discipline within a controlled and cultured manner to safely dream, create, explore or pioneer, in order to make present our imagined future.

If we are to progress, we must be able to dare to push the boundary of freedom in any field of a Journey Forward, be it in the family, the community, or the world. This is how we create value.

The Best Version of Ourselves

It is always necessary to create and develop a discipline of creating value, starting from self. We have to push the boundary of self-discipline towards becoming the best version of ourselves.

While the entire Journey to Bloom, of which this book is about, has been written with an individual growth in mind, I do believe these principles can also be applied to groups and entities. With this in mind, I emphasise that charity begins at home, and we cannot give what we do not have, otherwise trouble eventually catches up on us. Therefore it is necessary for us to build values by improving personal attitudes and skills toward being the best version of ourselves.

We have to begin from the self: very few people have succeeded in ever impacting the world positively without a sincere experience and mastering of the self. Tinkering about the edge is a gradual physical, mental, psychological and spiritual migration of purpose across margins and to the fringes, in order to influence our external environment.

We gain the benefit of influence and movement by developing a non-complacent attitude around any settled domain. This is what brings out our individual uniqueness, and as P.T. Barnum said, *"No one ever made a difference by being like everyone else."*

To move, we have to be unique, and to be unique, we have to recognise mediocrity as the enemy and maintaining the status quo as a villain.

Value Through Life's Circumstances

We can also capitalise on events and circumstances surrounding our lives to progress in our Journey Forward. Circumstances such as changing career, having a baby, starting a business, relocating, going to college, achieving a higher educational degree or any endeavour which is taken from a position of strength and wanting more, may be circumstances through which we develop deliberate processes for progress in order to succeed.

Life at the Edge

Creativity happens at the edge of life, but staying at the edge is a risky process. It demands courage and tact because, at the edge, you tinker with ideas which have either not been figured out or are only now being discovered.

Sometimes these ideas are difficult for others to understand, but when one makes a success out of them, they yield massive rewards, which in turn builds confidence and expands one's wave of influence.

Fortune Favours the Bold

Lasting creativity which happens at the edge does not happen through coercion, it happens through influence. However, I believe it is not possible to easily push the boundaries of influence without first 'breaking rules'.

This is because the established system works by preserving the status quo, and a perfect alignment with the System destroys any chance of innovation.

Crafting a creative culture entails breaking barriers, and this disruption which innovation and creativity brings is always one step ahead of the orderliness of rules and regulations. The System thrives through conformance but creative protagonists are willing to venture by leaving their comfort zone.

There is lots of uncertainty at the edge. Anyone who wants to achieve something meaningful must move to the edge and stir the settled pot of an established System. This is dangerous, but fortune favours the bold. An ancient African proverb says, '*A timid soul cannot attain to the influential stake of his clan.*'

Tinker from a Position of Freedom

The danger which arises from stirring the pot supports my stance that the risk of successful creativity is better implemented when you have attained the freedom of the Journey Forward rather than through the chaos of the Journey Back, for two reasons.

Firstly, it should not take place within an unknown, uncontained or unestablished terrain, and secondly, you should not stake all you have on it, despite the temptation to do so, even with the conviction of your innovation.

The art of 'tinkering' must be accompanied by careful risk management and analysis of potential consequences with the use of memory, mindfulness, and all prior learning. Without starting from a relatively solid foundation, you risk ruin and the possibility of spiralling back into the Journey Back.

Between Orderliness and Creativity

This is the reason why I believe a working society should consist of the right balance between preserving the System and encouraging creativity and innovation. The System must make space for entrepreneurship and creativity rather than preserving power through conformance.

The best innovators and change makers I have seen are those who first understand the norm and first engage in the discipline of keeping them before attempting to break them. For you to break rules successfully you must already have been highly adept at keeping rules efficiently, for working within boundaries allows you to identify weaknesses. From here you can create and build within boundaries in order to move them. The System ought to make allowances for this so that it is not overwhelmed.

Principle 10: BLOOMING – Tinker about the Edge

Creativity: Between the Liberals and Conservatives

While it may not be very clear-cut, let us divide those who are in favour of the preservation of the System as conservatives, and those who would want to push the boundaries as liberals (I am not using these terms in a political sense).

Liberals and conservatives are both right, but there will always remain a conflict between the liberals and the conservatives. Liberals want to break barriers and conservatives want to preserve them. Denial is tragic, delay is deadly.

The solution is in moving forward rationally. For the liberals to realise that wishes are not horses. Foresights and insights must have a firm root in culture and trends. Denial of the reality will be tragic for the liberal, delay of the action will be deadly for the conservative.

It is for the creative liberals to understand preservation, and as Newton said, *'if I can see much afar, it is because I am resting on the shoulder of giants.'* We have to collectively refine, reform and build on precedents and avoid the temptation to throw away the past as a trash worthy of being forgotten.

It is also for the conservatives to realise that the law of entropy is incompatible to the good old days: there is no going back, the way of progress is forward.

Together liberals and conservatives should reimagine in multitude, allow that which would decay do so; build on systems which work and let them thrive through continual creativity.

To have arrived at this point of the Journey Forward is to have come to an understanding of the entropic nature of life; knowing nothing is static. From this awareness, we cannot afford to stake our life on the perpetual workability of a System or process if no creative work is applied. There is only one constant, which is change. So, we can say, the only workable way is to Journey Forward.

But you ought to be sure of what you are doing before rocking the boat and pushing boundaries because pushed too far there could be a backlash. Be sure you can handle its consequences before you venture. If you are not ready, forces in the System are waiting ready to spiral you back to the slavery of the Journey Back.

You cannot stop here though, like the cyclist, you know the only way is 'forward', and so, armed with your self-awareness, be courageous and strategic. As Nelson Mandela said, *'It always seems impossible until it's done'*. So, just do it!

Talking of Nelson Mandela, I shall show other historical figures who have used courage and creativity and have in the process changed the world for the better.

Historical Examples of Tinkering About the Edges

Marco Polo tinkered deep through the edges of his Venetian environment when he embarked on a 25,000 km trip across Asia where he visited dozens of great cities. He acquired great cultural influences and after his return created a great epic chronicle of his travels. This became the basis for what all Europeans knew about the Orient for many years to come and inspired others to make similar journeys. He broke down many barriers across the Silk Road.

Christopher Columbus developed a plan to seek a western sea passage to the East Indies, hoping to profit from the lucrative spice trade, and following persistent lobbying in multiple kingdoms, he received sponsorship from Queen Isabella I and King Ferdinand II. When Columbus left his European boundary in August 1492 and completed four voyages across the Atlantic

Ocean, opening the way for the widespread European exploration and colonization of the Americas. His expeditions were the first known European contact with the Caribbean, Central America, and South America, and it inaugurated a period of exploration, conquest, and colonization that lasted for centuries, thus bringing the Americas into the European sphere of influence.

For many reading this book, it is far easier to be creative than it was for these people back in history: all you need is a workable laptop or phone with internet and you have the entire world to play with and discover.

For instance, in our time, Elon Musk is focusing on the vision for establishing a permanent human colonization and settlement on Mars: an idea extensively explored in science fiction is becoming an actualisation through the creativity of man.

Education and Creativity

To be successful in Principle 10 and to tinker about the edge, it requires a great deal of knowledge and experience, and the tool towards this is education.

Jean Piaget, the Swiss psychologist says, *"The principal goal of education in the schools should be creating men and women who are capable of doing new things, not simply repeating what other generations have done."*

Education ought to be more than acquiring formal learning, it should lead us to the edge of initiative where we are able to develop specific knowledge.

The more the System is willing and able to sustain this environment where people can confidently take risks and create, the more developed the System itself becomes.

On the part of the student, there has to develop a passion for learning. Once this passion to learn and understand becomes ingrained, then it becomes a tool for building knowledge and wisdom, borne of personal life experiences, travel, exposure and tested observational intuition.

Apply Creativity to Develop Value and Uniqueness

At this stage of our journey, we want to know how to do something which society cannot yet easily do or train other people to do. It is a devoted search for this uniqueness where we acquire power and can gain influence.

This is easier than imagined because all we have to do is be ourselves and follow after our innate talent, genuine curiosity and passion. If we can discover ourselves in this manner, and dare to remain ourselves, we will thrive.

When we have come through all the stages of experiences described in previous chapters, it becomes easier for us to be authentic. There are disordered characters in society who believe they are authentic, but they have not followed the process. They have not bloomed from chaos and have not mastered gratitude. They have not sustained focus on their purpose or indeed have not found their purpose. We must continue to be grateful, honour memory, value motherhood and practice mindfulness to ensure we are not, too, living falsely.

Between Rationality and Tinkering

Taking risks is not our natural default setting. Neurologists generally agree the evolutionary development of our brain is wired toward avoiding harm. But a number of developed Systems (such as the legal system), especially in developed countries, have been useful at relatively mitigating the downward effect of risks which accompany the venture of 'tinkering about the edges' thus encouraging creativity so much that the idea of pushing boundaries is taken as a natural step.

We are living in an age where the gap between what can be imagined and what can be accomplished has never been smaller.

Most of us have the potential to tinker at a far lower risk than our ancestors did. For instance, when our ancestors went on the quest for a new land; coupled with the danger of malevolence from fellow Sapiens, they were in danger of being hunted by wild beasts, in danger of unknown diseases and ailments, and without the promising medications against viruses and bacteria as we have today.

Now, many of us do not require to undergo the perilous danger of having to travel around the Silk Road or across the Atlantic, nor need the permission of any King or Kaiser in order to achieve creative feats. The internet has changed the world in multiple dimensions.

I believe the world is at the dawn of a shift towards new freedom, but this new age, born of tinkering at the edges may leave multitudes who have not already started making this Journeys behind. To arrive at it you still have to follow a process, albeit non-linear, through a personal journey of discovery.

Risk Assessment

Creativity is a high-risk, high-return strategy. Even with education, there is the temptation to go beyond boundaries without having an adequate analysis and assessment of the risks involved. Whoever succeeds would need to balance creativity with the management of the risk involved.

Risk management is a systematic method of identifying and controlling areas or events which have potential for causing unwanted change, either by elimination, mitigation, or by building contingency against them.

Risk management identifies as many risk events as possible, minimises their impact, manages responses to those events that do materialise, and provides contingency to cover risk events that actually materialise.

Risk management either of a process or a situation should not only be limited to business development, product design or project management, but should be a bedrock of life decisions.

Managing risk should not be the antithesis of creativity but it should be the essence of creativity. It should apply to every facet of our lives amidst its volatility, complexity, uncertainty and ambiguity. The first function of our creative endeavours should be a consideration of safety because our altruism will not protect us from ruin.

To manage risks we must exercise discipline by carefully assessing our plans and by not recklessly exposing ourselves.

Start small. While you may not succeed in magnitudes from this small entity, you can begin to build a responsibility into your wider circle of influence, which is what risk assessment is also about.

Take risks, but do not bite in a chunk. Take care you don't bet all at once or you will be trapped. Test the logic of your ideas in an incremental manner.

Maybe you are influenced by the success stories of others who have achieved and have become successful. It may appear they have had overnight success, but do you fully understand their

Principle 10: BLOOMING – Tinker about the Edge

journey, and their circumstances? Their journey is not yours; you must carefully consider your unique circumstance and apply any risk control which is necessary.

An Experience

Discovering purpose and building conviction may need the arm of fate. Developing confidence for this purpose may take years, and building this purpose into actualisation requires grit beyond this realm.

Having a dream is one thing, actualising that dream is another, but when you really have a dream, you do realise you have no option and there is no going back.

This is what Nietsche meant when he said, *"When you have a why, you will bear almost any how."*

I decided to take a personal risk some years back which involved a tinker about the edge: I had ideas on what I wanted to do with my life but I was locked into an unfulfilling, dreadful job out of necessity. In spite of my intense desire to quit and follow my dream, the reality of feeding my family took priority.

It was a long Journey Back and it was not easy having to stay put in an unfulfilling career. I made a trade-off from the onset. I was to be average, and I accepted a low-paid unfulfilling career, to create space and build value and uniqueness for my dream. I tinkered for years at the edge before I got a breakthrough into actualising my dream.

The non-aligned would pay the price for the tyranny of conformists. The more my dream tended to reality, the more daring I became until I became confident enough to break out of this unfulfilling career and progress my dream into a reality.

From all this, I would say, the rule of thumb should be, to risk assess the consequences of your creativity and of your tinkering about the edges. Is your purpose and dream strong enough to survive when the chips are down?

In Conclusion

To tinker about the edge is the route towards gaining power because of the unique specialism derived from putting creativity and innovation into play, and it is not for the faint-hearted.

Life moves forward and the man who lives life with integrity gains power. The next principle will discuss how to utilise power in order to sustain and make it lasting.

Practical Suggestions to Tinker around the Edge.

1. Make a list of your life goals - order them from the most important to the least
2. What is it differentiates you from others and aligns you with your passion?
3. How does your difference influence others?

PRINCIPLE 11.
BLOOMING – POWER IS SERVICE FOR UNITY AND PEACE

You cannot bloom without the realisation of power for service and peace.

Francis Niyi Akinola

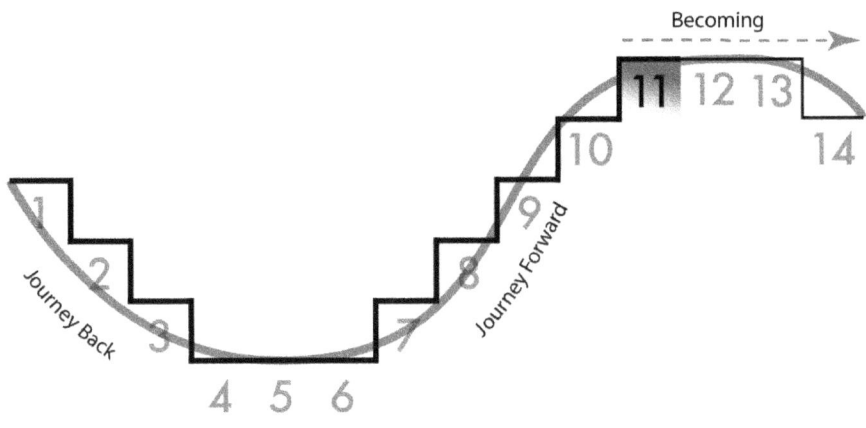

Principle 11

Principle 11: BLOOMING – Power is Service for Unity and Peace

As we spoke in the previous Principle, if you can *tinker about the edge* successfully, you will become master of your entity, the consequence of which is the accumulation of power within any domain.

This 4th milestone of the Journey Forward is the realisation of power. Here, we have something built and we are concerned with what has been built.

Power comes at a cost. As you progress, you begin to realise how power is a trial and a responsibility. A trial because all eyes are on you and in some sense, for and against you. Every step and decision of yours has consequences and is continuously scrutinized by all. A responsibility because from this point, your power has got to be utilised in service in order to keep intact what has been achieved or entrusted.

For the self, the goal of the Journey Forward is to become, and you cannot become without the utilisation of power for service in order to achieve or sustain peace; be it at work, in the family, in community or in any endeavour. Whatever the task it must be under power for service.

Meaningful and Lasting Power is a Service

Ultimately, in my opinion, I believe unless we lose ourselves in service to others, there is little purpose to our own lives. In a

Darwinian environment (talking evolution) it is often connived that 'might is right'. That is, you can conclude that in such a chaotic and complex system as ours, the only utility for getting things done is to attain to this power, and use power as a 'behaviourist' mechanism towards changing things.

To control a System, *'might may be right'*, but it surely does not last. Sustenance of power actually demands continual rising above the temptation of coercive control in order to complete the self-actualising Journey.

The Person at the Top

At this point, the successful utilisation of creativity along the edge has meant you have attained responsibilities to lead, and as such, you focus more on leadership and on the preservation of the System.

Here, you have become all which you were uncomfortable with and which you have criticised during your Journey Back. Now, those watching are waiting to see how you are going to manage the game.

The universe also watches how successful you are at conforming to truth, as this is what keeps your domain going.

Command the Heights

I have a valuable description which portrays my idea of leadership and how the execution of power could be utilised, not only to become but also to preserve the System in relation to reality, which to me appears to be the meaning of our human endeavours.

We act in order to become, and we work and engage with life with the hope that our endeavour will align with reality.

Principle 11: BLOOMING – Power is Service for Unity and Peace

Money, family, friends, knowledge, etc., are just tools to aid with this conformance. I shall dwell more on these in the next three Chapters.

Pyramids

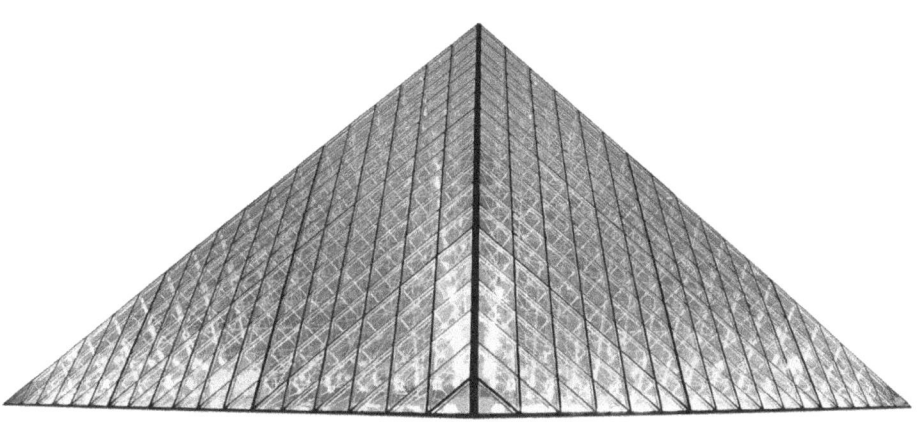

Louvre - Paris

The Louvre in Paris and the Great Pyramid of Egypt have something in common: they are both pyramids. Pyramids are representative of descending rays of the sun, which in some sense depicts the care which an idealistic leader has over their entity.

The person who controls a domain can be described as one who looks from the top of a pyramid and sees the big picture and is therefore better placed to exercise judgement on that domain. This is leadership.

Now, as we zoom in closer to observe the detail of the Louvre we see an array of triangular panes mapped above one another.

With regards to our description, we can say whosoever is at the tip of any of these individual triangular domains leads and governs the triangle (domain) which in turn sits upon another triangle (domain). These leaders are themselves a subject of a much broader triangular pane, until on very tip of the pyramid sits the apex entity which governs every other subordinate triangle.

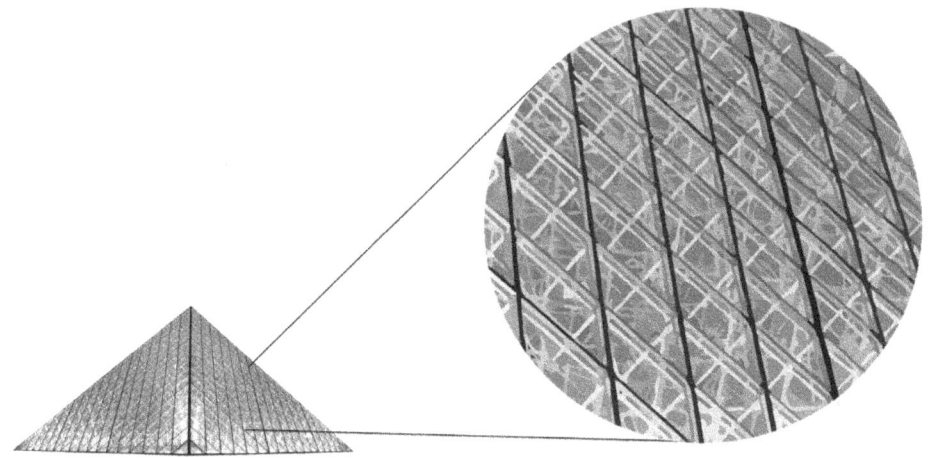

Detailed Structure of a Pyramid

It is debatable whether on a human level, if anyone, or group sits on this broad apex, which is actually, the tip of the pyramid.

The real challenge in our times is to decide who has this ultimate control, or whether it is beneficial for anyone to have ultimate control, recognising its high-end risk of responsibility and ruin.

Whereas, the usurping of this tip constitutes the current global political strife and the current play of the survival of the fittest, which sadly, is a regression back into the medieval rather than progression.

A Culture of Don't Ask Don't Tell

The Romans once had a culture where the emperor was not only a servant of the gods but was himself a god, this was until the entire Roman empire collapsed.

There was once a similar idea in my culture during the reign of the Oyo Empire, where the king is known to be an intimate associate of the gods and he is answerable to no one. This capturing of the apex and controlling everything controllable is a temptation to where man has always aspired but this is an ideal beyond capture.

There will always be external threats where someone stronger would conquer the domain governed, or internal strife which could fracture the entire fabric of the pyramidal unit, opening it up to being taken over by others.

Competition is Real But Must be Healthy

This multi-layered pyramidal system on the one hand shows the evolutionary nature of the survival of the fittest, as bigger triangles absorb the smaller ones.

We are competitive by nature, but unguided competition collapses the entire pyramidal edifice. Competition by nature has a bent towards being an endless *zero-sum* game when manifested through ego and status boosting.

The debased mind would take advantage at conquest towards self-aggrandizement and personal survival. But no one eventually survives an unguided competition. The winner will ultimately be overcome by another higher power and he becomes part of somebody else's precipice. In economics we say 'human needs are endless' it is the same with power, it is an endless struggle.

In many countries for instance, market policies are developed and structured in such a manner which fosters a healthy competition. The result of this is the growth of entities which strive to master each other.

We have also as a species been able to tame these struggles by channelling our unpleasant energies into the altruistic benefits of sport. Sport is an ingenuity of modern times, where competition exists with limited risk but with high reward.

Power's Ultimate Usefulness Lies with Service

Might may be right in the short term, but it has an ephemerality to its tale. This culture of survival of the fittest is not a timeless strategy, nor a tool for self-actualisation.

We find the entire history of humanity littered by this struggle politically, economically, socially and even spiritually. Mankind's nature of a warlike pursuit, survival at all costs, can be, and is being controlled by the entity which governs the pyramidal hierarchy.

Considering the depiction of power from an hierarchical pyramidal perspective as we have been discussing, we see how in many places, the allure of status and the corresponding charm that power brings has caused the attempt to level up chains of command to be very daunting despite its vivid calamitous consequences when this is not done.

We can assume that anyone at the top of the hierarchy would not want his precipice to falter because he knows he would crumble with it, so he would do all he can to preserve the integrity of the pyramid under his control.

Using might to fight your way to the top will ultimately be a burden and ordeal in futility. One may assume competition against other pyramids (or triangles) to be right, but the ultimate winner would be he who can preserve order, unity and peace through service, across the entire hierarchy of pyramids. To be contented, you would have to win across the globe and the universe. That is impossible for man, but there is another way.

Life will be chaotic for any leader who does not expend power in service for unity and peace, because he will not be able to preserve the centre and hold things in unison.

Principle 11: BLOOMING – Power is Service for Unity and Peace

The Risk of Leadership

It is difficult to sustain the forward and expansive motion of any institution amidst the experiences of their journeys back and forth (within this realm of the survival of the fittest) without the utilisation of power as a tool of service, so that perhaps there may be peace and unity.

As Harper Lee says, '*A court is only as sound as its jury, and a jury is only as sound as the men who make it up.*' There is a deep symbiosis which takes place between the leader and the led and it is up to the leader of a domain to lead authentically and serve the entity in order to build up good people in the process and to ensure wise judgements are collectively made towards the progress and benefit of such entity, thus ensuring its unity and preventing its collapse.

Going back to using the Louvre pyramid scenario, we can preserve a benign, well-aligned stream of care and governance of subordinate triangles by assuring (to the best of our abilities) we are committed to fairness, equity and the well-being of everyone through the decisions we make and in the actions we take. This service sure demands a lot of responsibility.

Leadership is always a risk, and the burden of authentic leadership lies in the care and sustenance of the respective domain. If the leader does not serve to preserve the unity of the entity under his care, then this entity collapses.

To move and not stall, we have to learn the act of leadership, which has little to do with a social position, but is about developing a mindset of care and responsibility for the people in relation to a cause.

Leadership, nowadays, also can mean, not just those who have an immediate obligation towards others, but on a broader note, a leader is someone who has a goal worthy of a calling which would be beneficial to humanity.

On this broader note, a leader is someone who wishes and works for the peace and well-being of all within the pyramid, irrespective of their position within the physical hierarchy, because he is aware that the collapse of any domino puts him at risk. The leader has the double responsibility of serving and sustaining this system which he has either created or inherited.

Leadership is an understanding of unity and peace as the prerequisite for a sustainable domain, not the physical hustle for superiority.

One who wishes and works for the peace, unity and well-being of all, is actually a person on top of every hierachy.

Peace is the summit of man's endeavour. Every political, social and religious organization, at least in theory, claims to be on the side of peace. It is also the big focal point of many Nobel Prizes. Talk is cheap since the led are not fooled. Peace has to be pragmatic.

Working for peace is not just about championing reconciliation, it is also the organisation, order creation and sustainable system maintenance for the service of the led, in spite of the chaotic nature of humanity and its environment.

The Motive of Power

The opportunity for power lies in its potential to become, and we cannot become without developing a mindset devoted to service and peace.

Power has the tendency of being viewed from a negative perspective. When we think of power, we immediately assume greed and personal acquisitions, because for many, the idea of power is an opportunity for greed. An idea warped inordinately by the ineptitude examples of many leaders throughout history.

It is not so much that power lacks altruism but that its allure is so captivating that it easily ignores restraint and draws much of its recipients deep down through its negative drawbacks.

Many appear to succeed by the allures of position and possession using the tool of falsity, force and coercion to achieve their purpose, but eventually these stall, become depleted and incapable of moving anyone forward anymore. The domain then dries up and the misuse of power ultimately kills it off.

Preserving Structure and Processes

I have no little tale of such power failures from my native country, Nigeria, but I have come to experience this human flaw not through personal circumstance but by observing any System which fails to work on preserving peace through effective structure and efficient processes.

People are all alike everywhere, and leadership makes a huge difference to the thriving of a domain and for preserving a culture of commitment to written justice and creativity.

Power, for many, is about position and possession, yet, its real effectiveness lies in its ability to build institutions and people, to voluntarily influence in a positive direction for the welfare of the people.

This capacity to influence is what propels every protagonist, good or bad and this is what every leader or ruler craves, rightly or otherwise. The capacity to influence was the domain of Abraham Lincoln, Martin Luther King Jr., Mahatma Ghandi and Mother Teresa; this is why they were so successful.

The Challenge in a Power for Service and Peace

It is important not to trivialize the difficulty that lies in leadership by service toward peace.

A servant leader is not naïve and weak, He senses every external and internal chaos about his domain and uses them as an opportunity for growth.

Humans are a complex entity. Experienced and truthful leadership of people which is devoid of any greedy ulterior motives is becoming more in short supply.

The temptation for many leaders is to give up on humanity under the pretext of complexity which surrounds it. For instance, many business leaders are increasingly opting for technology instead of human beings, not primarily because of efficiency, but because people are complex and difficult to manage.

Machines will not complain and will do what you want them to do. Human beings will ask for more pay, sick leave, extra bonus, and employment benefits, and if you dare take any unusual step, they will accuse you of racism, misogyny, discrimination, welfare rights etc. We humans are a complex species.

Community leadership forms the grassroots of our society and civilisation, but more daunting than entrepreneurial activities is community building because it relies on working with people and comes with little or no financial recompense. It can only be effective as a call and vocation.

As someone actively involved in business and community building, I agree community building is one of the most challenging aspects many leaders may experience. Task management is hard enough, money management is harder, but people management, to the extent of building a cohesive and integrated community is

Principle 11: BLOOMING – Power is Service for Unity and Peace

one of the great challenges of our cultures, but I must say it is the most rewarding.

Gathering people of different beliefs and idiosyncrasies and maintaining them not to fail in this unpredictable world is a huge challenge. Man's complexity is what frustrates many leaders and what lures them down the path of tyranny.

In many corporations, most people in HR have become detached enforcers, and while employees notice the underlying hypocrisies, talents are increasingly lost in organisation, while companies as a whole increasingly prefer machines and technologies as an escape from the unstable nature of man. What is this unstable nature of man like? It is like the differing viewpoints in this tale of 'The Man, his Son and his Donkey.

The Man, his Son and his Donkey

Once there was a father who decided to travel to a distant land with his son. He prepared a donkey and they set off.

The father started the journey by walking along while he let his son ride the beast. After sometime, they arrive at village where one of the villagers commented about how arrogant and disrespectful the young son was, because he comfortably rides on the donkey while his father was walking under the sun. He opined, *"If he has a little sense he must have given way for his father to ride the donkey because he is the younger and stronger man."*

The father and his son heard this and decided to exchange position. The son gets off the donkey and allowed his father to ride and off they went on their journey.

Another villager came across them and commented *"What an irresponsible, selfish father this man was. He rides comfortably on the donkey while letting his son to walk under the heat of the sun. As a parent he must act as a model of justice and compassion to his child."*

The father felt ashamed of the situation, and wanting to please both the first and second advisors, he got off from the donkey and compassionately joined his son in walking along with their donkey.

Soon after, they met with another villager who commented *"Look at how stupid these guys are, bringing with them a donkey and not riding on it. What's the point of having that donkey all along?"*

Upon hearing this, the father and the son felt they were looking like a bunch of fools walking all the way with a vacant

The Man Carrying his Donkey

mighty transportation beast uselessly following them. So they decided to ride together in the donkey as they continue with the journey.

They met another villager who commented *"How merciless and abusive these guys are. Both of them cared to ride the poor donkey, haven't they realized that they are heavy enough for the lowly beast."*

They felt deeply sorry for the donkey and so both of them got off the donkey and carried the heavy beast on their backs instead, as they continue to their journey slowly and foolishly as they ever may seem.

Everyone looked and ridiculed them for their foolishness. So end the story of a man who would like to please everyone, every time and all at once.

It is a misconception that servant leadership is meant to appease everyone. This may be a fool's errand such as this tale. A man who is afraid of any confrontation and is bent on pleasing everyone cannot serve as a leader.

To make peace, it does not mean a leader must be timid and afraid of controversies. In all, one must be true to oneself, and if we make a mistake in the process, we should remember, we are after all like everyone else, we are flawed.

To be a servant leader is to be a friend of humanity and to be able to deal with all the idiosyncrasies surrounding this. It is no use running away from such responsibility if one would proceed on this Journey. If here, we seek at all cost to avoid controversies, we shall eventually lose and come to ruin.

We ought to purify our motives and if we fail, our conscience will be there to attest to our altruism that we came to this struggle to serve and unite, not to self-aggrandize and ruin the System.

This ruin is depicted in an ancient tale from an African hinterland brought about by a man who is the polar opposite of the man with the donkey who would please all. This man fears neither god nor man, he used might to attain to leadership and tried to circumscribe the responsibility of dealing with man's idiosyncrasies.

The Tale of a Brass Drum

Once upon a time in a town called Jogbo. An elected king was told by the chieftains of the need to take an ancestral vow and enter a pact of service of the people, according to an age-old traditional pact between the citizens and their king before he could ascend the throne.

The pact consist of a little ceremonial ritual using a brass drum and a brass crown which commits kings to a long and peaceful reign of servitude devoid of self-aggrandisement.

This crony king elect did not take kindly to this. He cheated his way through the process by not undertaking the pact.

He eventually got to be king and ruled by fear and tyranny. He became very insecure about his position and was very autocratic as a result.

His reign was filled with political struggle, and was defined by wastage and opulence. He refused any advice to reform and got rid of any opposition at the slightest provocation.

His main opposition, consisting of human rights activists, got hold of an age long secret through which they could get rid of him as king:

As the king did not go through the pact process and did not make the required vow, any initiate who beat the brass drum

Principle 11: BLOOMING – Power is Service for Unity and Peace

The Brass Crown and Brass Drum

while the king wore his brass crown would lead to the king suffering from migraine and eventually die.

The opposition carefully crafted a plan. They waited patiently for an opportunity for the king to wear his brass crown. It finally occurred during one of the town's grandest ceremonies. The initiate drummer snuck in with other normal drummers in the town. While the festive drumming and dancing were on, the initiate drummer began to beat the brass drum.

The King at first began to feel discomforted, then it resulted into headache, then migraine. As the festivities continued, no one could tell what was causing the king's discomfort. They watched their tyrannical king struggle helplessly with migraine until he slumped and died.

The moral here is, the king must be the prime servant, not the people. This tale was turned into an African political movie called *Saworoide* directed by Tunde Kelani.

Becoming a Rare Breed

Serving people and meeting their expectations is daunting, but you have travelled this far not because power has been thrust on you, but because you have earned it and have built some experience to serve in the process.

It is said, *'it is lonely at the top'* this is because only a few people manage to find their way meaningfully up there, but here you are, one out of many. This is why you have embarked on your quest, so utilise it in order to learn and become.

Authentic leaders are not only in short supply but are being awaited by a multitude of people looking for inspiration and good examples. We are doomed as a species if we do not have a sufficient supply of them. To become, you cannot deal solely with machines, you inevitably deal with men.

From Leadership towards Unity and Peace

There are no problems that we cannot solve together, and very few that we can solve by ourselves; but to be together, we need a relationship. When we are able to manage relationships appropriately there will be no impossibilities.

Without a responsible leadership that is aware of the necessity of inclusivity, it would be impossible to initiate a humble, broadminded relationship, devoid of sentimental compartmentalization out of which any hierarchical domain fragments.

Principle 11: BLOOMING – Power is Service for Unity and Peace

If we do not Journey with a mindset of service for the sake of peace, we become brittle-minded and spiral back into the struggle of Journey Back, which is harder work.

We Bloom to Become

By becoming successful at *tinkering about the edges*, we attain to a power, of which its utilization is about developing authentic leadership, which is in turn about service towards the preservation of a peaceful integration of the domain being led.

So, we may ask, after power what happens next? The real purpose of our engagement is not to acquire, it is to become, and to become, we would need a power exit plan to *'get out of the way'*.

This *'getting out of the way'* is not about squandering what we have attained, it is about consolidating them without losing out on the stake of what has been achieved and passing on the baton to the next leader.

Abundant worlds of vision and possibility await, especially once we have attained selflessness. Then, the utilisation of power will preserve and enable us to become, which is what the final three Principles are about.

Practical Suggestions for Using Power for Service and Peace

1. Think of someone you have not been on speaking terms with in a while. How can you contact such a person and rebuild a relationship? Try and act upon this.
2. Be proactive in forming and leading a small team toward an altruistic project.
3. What proactive role do you play in supporting a group to which you belong? How does this act as a service?

BECOMING

The Becoming Principles

These Principles concentrate on how the ultimate purpose of man's fulfilment can be attained.

PRINCIPLE 12.
BECOMING - BUILD A LEGACY

I must be willing to give up what I am in order to become what I will be.

Albert Einstein

Blooming Through Chaotic Times

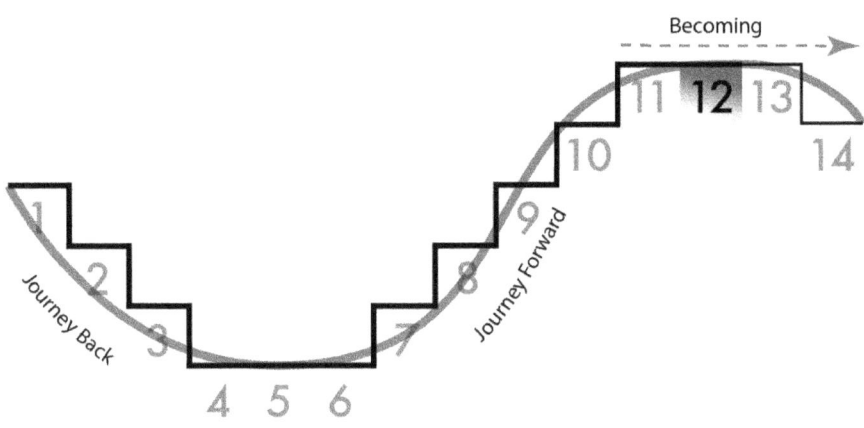

Principle 12

Principle 12: BECOMING – Build a Legacy

Building from the previous Principle, we can say, for anything good to come about, it's got to have a strong, passionate, inspiring and dynamic leadership which exercises power for service to achieve peace.

An authentic audacity is needed to integrate others in order to create a meaningful and impactful influence.

Becoming is real wealth. Life is worth living when we find meaning and voluntarily participate in what life does to the best of our ability.

What does life do? In a nutshell, life is involved in the business of giving. The entire universe is always in a state of giving, and it is out of being in synergy with this reality that a lasting legacy is birthed. As such, if we hope to become, we have to give and let go.

On The Balance between Purpose and Letting Go

If we have managed our journey successfully so far, we must have transcended deeper and found more meaning in living. Without the proactive utility of what I describe here, it is impossible to make meaning out of the entire chaos surrounding us.

Purpose is the bedrock of legacy because it births vision and entrenches meaning. The stronger and deeper such purpose the more lasting the legacy will be. Legacy, which consists in letting go, a letting-go which would be impossible unless a benevolent advantage of such gesture has been experienced.

We may not see what benefits accrue from letting go unless we have developed a capacity for broad-based universal goodness which gives without discrimination, and we cannot have the latter simply by gate-crashing our way to power without having embarked on the Journey Back which introduces an authentic Journey Forward.

A man with power can only let go if he is fortunate enough to have discovered a meaning beyond himself, and it is only then he can claim on building a legacy.

Our leaving legacy is about being fruitful, and the ultimate fruitfulness will be found in letting go. This is where we discover an ever-increasing touch with reality.

Power only decays when leaders refuse to voluntarily let go and they would also lose on the realisation of what truly sustains and thereby remain stuck. A powerful person who neither leaves nor lets go when necessity demands, will not discover the liberty which comes out of making oneself and others thrive by letting go. When you lose the fear of letting go, you truly begin to live.

The Go-Giver

Whoever has found a compelling enough purpose can give up anything which would hinder such fulfilment if clung to.

The *Go-Giver* written by Bob Burg and John David Mann echoes this.

It is the story of Joe, an ambitious salesman who came across a legendary consultant called Pindar who introduced him to a series of 'go-givers' who shared their success stories and from where he discovered the 5 Laws of Stratospheric Success which introduced him to potent power which lies in giving.

From these encounters, Joe discovered that the point is ultimately not what we do or what we accomplish, but what we become by giving, pushing us towards an accomplished becoming.

Putting others first and continually adding value to others ultimately is the summit of a fulfilled life because here, you don't lose by giving, you realise how giving what you have is an act of receiving.

Pindar says, *"Every giving can happen only because it is also ultimately a receiving …. And we have to be open to this receiving too…"* The key to effective giving is to stay open to receiving. The universe reciprocates a generous cheerful giving of one's value without expectation but with an open gracious heart to receive.

Givers Gain®

Ivan Misner, Greg Davies, and Julian Lewis further explored this concept in their book *Infinite Giving*. Using the 7 principles of Givers Gain®, a phrase credited to and popularised by Ivan Misner, they showed how strength and influence lie in giving.

Life is a game. It does feel good to be winning a game but when we are winning, it is unlikely we want the game to end. However, if everyone loses at the expense of your winning, you eventually end up having no one to play with.

So, the secret lies in keeping the game going by enabling everyone to have sufficient means and enthusiasm with the prospective means for thriving such that they would want to want to continue to play the game. This is called a win-win.

What is Legacy?

Legacy (and philanthropy) is what has been developed by any individual, which becomes of benefit to others; and the more unselfish this is, the longer it lasts.

Philanthropy does have a bad press; this is because everyone has become self-acclaimed philanthropists towards maintaining wealth, status, or power. Today, giving has been tainted by selfish ulterior motives.

Margaret Thatcher, former British Prime Minister once said, *"Being powerful is like being a lady. If you have to tell people you are, you aren't."*

I would argue the same applies to Philanthropy. If you tell everyone you are a Philanthropist, it is probably not authentically so.

Moving up to this phase demands giving and letting go of our acquired resources, not because we simply have to, but because we are devoted to giving and we can see the benefits this giving acquires, not only to others but also to ourselves.

How Shall we Give?

We can make a virtue of necessity from compulsive giving, but if giving is forced, rather than voluntarily embraced, it may communicate limited effectiveness and detract from the satisfaction which comes from spontaneous giving.

How often we have, for instance, been compelled to pay taxes which we would rather not want to pay? What if we try to understand and embrace the reason why we ought to pay? 'What is in it for us' is a natural and necessary question to ask by the giver. This question is not necessarily selfish.

Principle 12: BECOMING – Build a Legacy

Anyone who has travelled this far knows from experience that giving is a loving and creative act. Giving gets. Givers gain. But giving at this stage is about discovering a meaningful delight in letting go of knowledge and possession without the expectation of a magical result or instant compensation.

We can only see this reason if we assume the attitude and mindset of a leader. It buttresses my argument that our reluctance to give is an educational and experiential one. The joy from giving is maximised when we cultivate a mindset which is broad and deep enough to take up responsibility for everything, yet without being overwhelmed by anything.

Life can only take full meaning when it is lived for others, then we are on the path to building a lasting legacy. Our mission is to spread this novelty, so that through us it may reach everyone, even long after we are gone.

It is also okay to have reluctance. If it was easy to give, perhaps the returns would not be as great. I also do not think anyone should have to be compelled to give under compulsion unless there is already a social contract in place to give (such as taxes). The real motive to give -more often than not- must be voluntary, and its best effect is felt, not just because we can give, but because we realize why we give.

Between Entropy and Reality

In order to better clarify the need to give, I will introduce a very important concept about the nature of reality.

Entropy is a quantity from the 2nd Law of Thermodynamics. This attribute may well be one of the most prolific open secrets of science regarding the nature of reality. It is a measure of disorder in a system. It can also be regarded as a measure of the amount of uncertainty or randomness in the system

Disorders are caused by an agitation of molecules, which produces heat from a point of lower disorder to a higher disorder. This phenomenon is called Entropy.

It is to be understood that, material-wise we are constituents of stars, and as such entropy is found in every created body.

Entropy is similar to energy, but a simple but clear difference between energy and entropy is: while you are in control of the former, the latter takes its toll whether you would like it to or not.

If we do not make a virtue of this necessity, tap into it and find meaning in it, it is almost always a most disappointing driver of meaninglessness, because, with entropy, we are not in charge.

Many have asked, what is the meaning of life? I would suggest: Life is entropic by nature. It is to be given up.

This disorder and decay are the eventual constants and nothing is permanent. In order words, it is not what you build but what you give up which eventually wins the day, and death shows that in a most poignant way.

The highest form of this letting go is death. We learn at the school of death, it is the biggest certainty. Even death provides the meaning of great strength (I shall talk more on my experience about this in the Afterword).

What Entropy Beckons for

We may either spend our days bemoaning the unfortunate nature of entropy or we may strive to derive meaning from it.

Whatever may have been won thus far from our journeying can only be sustained through a commitment to reality. Commitment to reality means we have to learn to let go of whatever we hold tight today.

Why should we let go? We should let go because this is what the entire creation does. This is the way to tap into the cosmic story. We derive meaning by tapping from nature's 'timeliness' through a collaboration with the universe in giving.

This is where love is born. Love is this act of giving and dying which the universe does: it breeds legacy.

Knowledge also Decays

We can say nature is the prey of entropy since this unwilled decay is the order of everything. It is not just about material decay; we can also talk mimetically about the immaterial aspect of entropy such as knowledge. For instance, we may often have to learn, unlearn and relearn in our quest to grasp our concept of reality. This process towards enlightenment can be viewed as being entropic in character.

All forms of knowledge give way. Science itself is a victim of entropy. It is said to advance one funeral at a time. Newtonian Law for instance, once a gospel of Physics, has been relegated in favour of Einstein's general Relativity.

Looking further back to the origin of humans, we see how Creationism was once the best explanation to explain how we came to exist on earth. In recent times, evolution and the theory of natural selection have clarified many ambiguous realities of living species, its nature and the environment.

I believe this premise of natural selection on which evolution theory is built, itself has an ambiguity which may be better clarified in the future by a better explanation, and as such, every theory is a susceptible victim of entropy. So, it is safe to say, knowledge: -isms, -ologies, and everything inbetween would also decay.

This does not mean that the person who does not learn is on the same par with the person who strives to understand reality. But any individual who learns must be humble enough to acknowledge the ephemerality of his knowledge, and that any scientific fact today may become obsolete tomorrow when won over by a better explanation about the nature of reality.

The quest for knowledge is a journey - not a destination - to reality. So, we may ask, what is reality?

What is Reality?

What is real? How do you define real? Reality - to use Swami Bhaktivedanta's definition, 'can be said to be an existence which cannot be vanquished. Something is real to the extent which it is able to withstand and sustain itself amidst every other factor.'

Idealistically, we can say reality is infinity. Life's purpose is achieved when we do our best to live in reality infinitely.

We must broaden our hearts and learn to be resilient in letting go, entering into the reality of giving as second nature in order to progress and live authentically.

We must continually practice free giving and letting go since, as I have shown from the analogy of entropy, nothing is more real than this giving and the summit of this reality is death. Giving is where ultimately life is derived. How? You may ask.

Money as Energy and Passion

It is important to discuss giving in monetary terms because it is an understandable means of exchange which we can easily measure and quantify. Giving in monetary terms is a real-time

Principle 12: BECOMING – Build a Legacy

test because of its tangibility and the application of rationality in the process.

I often observe money or currency, not only as a medium of exchange but holistically as the cumulative personification of the expenditure of energy in order to achieve an objective.

The physical, intellectual, emotional or spiritual utilisation of energy is what money signifies. Winston Churchill's famous wartime phrase engraved on the five-pound note catches well the significance of money as energy, it reads: 'I have nothing to offer but blood, toils, tears and sweat.'

When we have a passion, and we use this passion to discover purpose, and deepen our life experience by finding fulfilment in sharing (and giving up) our passion to others, we are indirectly 'spending money'. But we have to channel the utilisation of energy for the right cause:

First, we have to ensure we expend our energies for good aims.

Second, we have to ensure we do not acquire and use others' energies fraudulently. This is an unethical acquisition of money.

If you swindle anyone of their energies, 'entropy would take it back in a most calamitous manner, and we must know that entropy trumps energy.

Entropy Trumps Energy

Entropy trumps energy. What do I mean? Energy is our wilful utilization of money towards a certain end. Entropy is an unwilled snoop of money from us, because, even when we are reluctant to expend energy (money), forces beyond our control – sooner or later- expend this money of us, this is the nature of entropy. In relation to energy, we can say Entropy is the loss of energy to do work. A compelled work.

As such, money, if not used or spent, with time, becomes a victim of entropy which makes it useless and unsuitable for any meaningful venture. The push for money thus eventually becomes banal and to the ruin of the beholder.

This is why making money work for us is not the ultimate goal, we ought to find means of making it work for others too. Money is not a single-player game.

Between Building Community and Making Money

We all refer to life as being ultimately meaningful when it is lived for others, but we do not understand how and are unwilling to take up the risk. As Morpheus told Neo in The Matrix, there is a difference between knowing the path and walking the path.

It is innate in man to push outside oneself. We are social animals. This desire is what inspires us to want to create a family, be involved in the community, build a movement of people or join politics. Nature insists this of us, if we neglect this impulse, Nature ultimately seeks its pound of flesh.

There is more fulfilment for me in community and charitable work than in running a business. I would say though, despite community building being intrinsically fulfilling we need to survive and to do this we need money.

I advise that at the start of your journey, you need employment, and you need money to survive, so venturing into employment or business precedes community and charitable works, but many get stuck in the business of making money because of

Principle 12: BECOMING – Build a Legacy

the endlessness of human needs and they miss out on the more honourable process of moving on to build communities.

Maslow was right when he puts physiological needs at the base of motivation. Gusto is derived from giving out for the prospect of the other in order to build something new, not so much in taking from an established domain to benefit the self.

If we are not accustomed to giving early, it will become difficult to do so later in life. Eventually, we shall realise its banality and that its ultimate utility is when it is let go for the benefit of others. Voluntary community enterprise and Capitalism should go together.

I've often considered teaching and care-giving among the most fulfilling vocations one can have because while making money teachers and care-givers have a huge impact on people. Often they go above and beyond monetary expectations for those they teach.

The more we grow the more we discover teaching and caring as fundamental aspects and goals of human existence. I am sure there are many people, wealthy and otherwise, who have discovered the vocation of education and care: we can never know everyone motives for doing so.

Some Modern Examples of Giving

The following people have shown an extensive propensity for building legacy. However, I would like to mention that there are many people who give often in anonymity.

Mother Teresa is widely regarded as one of the most selfless and giving individuals in modern history. She dedicated her life to serving the poor and sick and provided care and compassion to people of all backgrounds and religions, and her legacy continues to inspire people around the world.

Oprah Winfrey is also a well-known for her donation to education, healthcare, and poverty alleviation programs, among others. She has also used her platform to promote charitable causes and inspire others to give back.

Malala Yousafzai has dedicated her life to promoting education and women's rights. She survived an assassination attempt by the Taliban in 2012 and has continued to advocate for education for all children, particularly girls.

While Bill Gates is known for his immense wealth, he has also given generously through the *Bill & Melinda Gates Foundation,* he has donated billions of dollars to support global health and reduce poverty.

Warren Buffett is known for his philanthropic efforts and has pledged to give away the majority of his wealth to charitable causes. In 2010, he and Bill Gates launched *The Giving Pledge,* which encourages other wealthy individuals to donate the majority of their wealth to charitable causes.

You Live and Leave a Legacy by Moving on and Getting Out of the Way

Of the last two examples I would like to discuss and draw some analogies. Whatever flaws he may have, I've always admired Bill Gates as one of the very few who have managed to find a way to reinvent and repurpose their life in order to move and not remain stuck in the Journey Forward. He is a typical example of moving on.

While he is best known as the co-founder of Microsoft, Bill Gates was able to reinvent himself from business into charity, running the Bill & Melinda Gates Foundation alongside his wife.

Bill Gates was creative enough to attempt a synergy between business and charity by championing a process which he terms creative capitalism, a system where wealthy individuals could give back to society by donating some substantial percentage of accumulated wealth to charities.

With the popularity of such ideas amongst Capitalists, we can see how altruism to the society and finding purpose in Community can trump a discovery of purpose which is entrenched solely in money and material acquisition.

Even more inspiring is the gesture of Warren Buffett, chairman, and CEO of Berkshire Hathaway. Buffett is not only one of the wealthiest people in the world, but he is also one of the most charitable, whereas, more than Gates, he also appears to be more aloof from his giving and about pushing on how his donation is spent.

In 2006, Buffett vowed to donate 85% of his wealth to the Bill and Melinda Gates Foundation, as well as other foundations set up by family members, and he does not seem to want to be the flag bearer of how his charity is spent. Gates still runs his Charity foundation, Buffett gave his money to Gates's charity and got out of the way of its consequential activism.

We may say it's okay for the likes of Bill Gates and Warren Buffett to give because they already have more than enough, and not many of us have that luxury. We may consider ourselves not having the capacity to dare to let go of the little we have.

While I agree that every financial giving calls for thriftiness, but giving is not about luxury, it's about attitude. One of my greatest inspirations for giving are not the wealthy and bountiful, they are the poor women in the interior villages of Africa who seem to understand giving and have ingrained hospitality and giving into their DNA. They are among the happiest people I've encountered, too. Strange how the world works. These women obviously need help themselves, but they never make any excuse for not giving.

Building a Lasting Legacy

What can exist long after we are gone? Is anything worthy of the name legacy at all?

Leaving a legacy starts with the discovery of a perpetual cause worth getting out of the way for, or you risk not living. A society reflects the nature of the legacy left by its predecessors in proportion to its relevance to truth and reality, so, instil your legacy and impart your knowledge to those who will be there after you let go.

Our inability to let go means we still possess potential yet to be actualised.

Money is good when sought ethically, but this, like every other thing, also vanishes. Only one thing lasts which is real: Love; and true love is about giving.

We are the best legacies to leave. When we make the best version out of ourselves, as described previously, we discover that everything we give simply points to the giving up of ourselves. We are personified potentials.

The process of giving ourselves means we become stories. The onus is then on us to do everything in such a worthwhile manner, to build a worthy monument of our existence and leave a meaningful footprint in the sand of time.

Only truth allows us to become progenitors for posterity. If this is not the essence of life amidst its meaninglessness, I do not know what is. We are a world of possibility if we have the courage to follow through with reality. We must master getting out of the way to reach the summit of the hierarchy of wisdom which is that of building a legacy. It is in learning to get out of the way we experience the fulfilment of beauty, joy and peace.

Principle 12: BECOMING – Build a Legacy

Practical Suggestions for Building a Legacy

1. Explore how much time, talent and treasure you give each week to others? Can this be increased?

2. Consider whether you give spontaneously or under compulsion? Develop a way to increase your spontaneous giving.

3. What little injustice have you fought over and have had to let go? Reflect on how letting go has improved your wellbeing.

Blooming Through Chaotic Times

PRINCIPLE 13. BECOMING - ITAKUN

*Try not to become a man of success.
Rather become a man of value.*

Albert Einstein

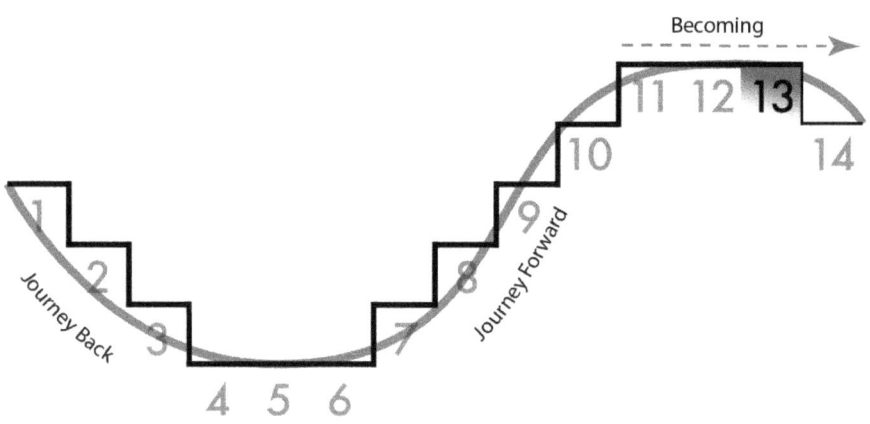

Principle 13

Principle 13: BECOMING – Itakun

The purpose of our questing is about becoming. What one discovers after being adept at generosity is the founding of oneself. This is what becoming is.

What is man? Who are we? What do we become out of the previous gesture? This is what I will attempt to describe.

Itakun is a Yoruba word which means strand. Itakun describes how everything is interlinked and everything is unity. The full expression is: Itakun to s'ogba, lo s'agbe, lo s'elegede!

This means, it is the same strand which produces the calabash, binds the gourd, and bounds the pumpkin. We take the description of these in turn.

Calabash, Gourd, and Pumpkin

Calabash, gourd, and pumpkin are all members of the Cucurbitaceae family and are often used interchangeably because they share similarities in terms of shape, size and use in various cultures.

Calabash is a term used to refer to several species of gourds with hard, durable shells that have been used for centuries to make a variety of objects, such as bowls, containers, musical instruments, and pipes.

Gourd is a term used to describe several species of plants that are related to cucumbers and melons. They can have a variety of shapes and sizes, including round, oval, or elongated, and can range in colour from green to yellow to orange.

Pumpkins are a type of gourd that is usually larger than other gourds, with a round or oblong shape and a bright orange colour. They have a thick, hard skin and a pulpy interior with seeds that are edible when cooked.

Pumpkins are used for a variety of purposes, such as for making pumpkin pies, soups, and bread. They are also used for decoration during the fall season, particularly during Halloween and Thanksgiving.

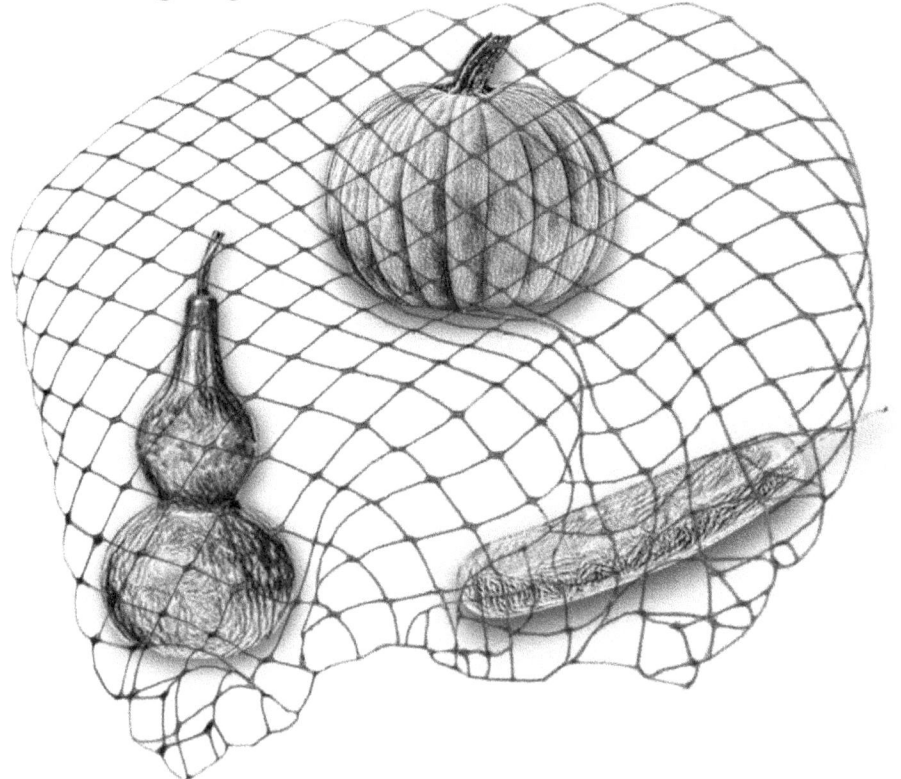

Calabash, Pumpkin and Gourd

Principle 13: BECOMING – Itakun

Pumpkins are also technically a gourd.

From the expression, *Itakun to s'ogba, lo s'agbe, lo s'elegede!* We say a pumpkin is technically a gourd and a calabash, since these are fruits of the same strand and are rooted, not just from the same species, but out of the same plant.

This full expression of Itakun finds an echo in many philosophies and cultures throughout the world. Itakun, using modern parlance can be best described as a Matrix.

So, why should we care? What is in it for us?

Itakun and the Matrix of Meaning

Matrix has definitions from multitudes of subjects yet most have similar connotations. Here are a few matrix definitions (in brief):

In Biology, the matrix can be described as the substance between cells or in which structures are embedded. They are fine materials used to bind together the coarser particles of a composite substance.

In Mathematics, the matrix is a rectangular array of quantities or expressions in rows and columns that is treated as a single entity and manipulated according to particular rules.

In Management, a matrix is an organizational structure in which two or more lines of command, responsibility, or communication may run through the same individual.

The Interconnectedness of Everything

One common factor in the description above is the interconnectedness of everything. Here we shall explore how every little action of ours is integral to mapping out who we are.

We discover this when we begin to give. We realise through an intimate study of our experience how life acts as a singular continuum and how we are unique from others yet the same as others.

The realisation in the individual of the interrelationship, interdependency, and interconnectedness of things and of actions brings to the fore the responsibility to balance and judge equitably.

When we realise how every act is dependent on us, we, in turn, realise how it affects the progress of any domain. If I am keenly aware that you are part of me, I will be less likely to do you harm.

This method of perception enables us to properly create the correct hierarchy of values and be able to judge appropriately and recognize a base unity out of our numerous diversities. In order to discover this, I shall revert to science once more.

The Interconnectedness of the Cosmos

Of course, we do not have to study science to have a full appreciation of the interconnectedness of everything. Experience is often better than study. However, the study of science allows us to discern subjective realities in an objective manner and offers us a platform to describe realities with better clarity.

From the Big Bang 13.7 billion years ago, matter, space, energy and time began. This we call Physics. From this, we are told 300,000 years after the Big Bang, matter and energy coalesced into complex structures of atoms and molecules, and their elemental interactions. The study of this process, we call Chemistry.

3.8 billion years ago, one remnant planet born of a supernova event of a star, created certain molecules which combined to form particularly large and intricate structures called organisms, from which you and I hail. The remnant planet is Earth and the study of organisms, we call this Biology.

From the study of physical realities, here we see how chemistry comes out of Physics and how Biology comes out of Chemistry. Humanity, including you and I, are constituents of this Biology. Scientifically, we are all products of the Big Bang.

From this little story, we can see how the 'Big Bang' strand has produced the universe which binds matter and energy and births organisms. Everything is interlinked, everything has a relationship, and everything is united.

Scientific Progress on Interdependency

This universal interdependency of everything was demonstrated by Albert Einstein's Theory of General Relativity. He shows how time and space are not mutually exclusive factors from matter.

In General Relativity, gravity is a curvature of space and time caused by the presence of mass and energy, and events occur in a continuous and deterministic manner, meaning every cause matches up to a specific, local effect. For instance, objects with mass and energy warp the fabric of space and time around them, creating a gravitational field that affects the motion of other objects nearby. The more massive an object is, the greater the curvature it creates in space-time and the stronger its gravitational field.

This relative effect as a result of gravity can be illustrated by imagining a bowling ball placed on a trampoline. The ball creates a curvature on the surface of the trampoline. If you place a smaller ball nearby, it will roll towards the larger ball because of the curvature, which in scientific terms also determines space-time, not space and time.

We have another theory which is not continuous, but only probabilistic and very uncertain yet quite relevant in describing our reality. It is called Quantum Mechanics.

Quantum Mechanics looks at the behaviour of matter and energy at their small and subatomic scales. It is a fundamental theory in modern physics, and it has led to many technological advances, including the development of the computer chip and the laser. At its core, quantum mechanics states that particles have both wave-like and particle-like properties and can exist in multiple states at the same time.

Currently, these two major pillars of physical realities, general relativity, and quantum mechanics, still exist mutually exclusive of each other (which contradicts Itakun). One of the highest goals of physics is to provide a complete and unified understanding of these two fundamental laws that govern our universe. This unifying principle is generally referred to as the *'Theory of Everything'*.

The *Theory of Everything* needs to reconcile these two theories, because Science's gut (and Itakun) tells her this relationship must exist, for, when we say everything is interdependent, how come we have two useful theories which are yet to have any relationship?

Between Science and Philosophy

This dichotomy between the two theoretical pillars of Physics finds relevance in the study of objective realities which is championed by science, and the study of humanities, as championed by Philosophy.

Science is a systematic and empirical approach to studying the natural world, relying on experimentation and observation to gather data and make predictions about how the world works.

Principle 13: BECOMING – Itakun

Philosophy, on the other hand, is a more abstract and conceptual approach to understanding reality, relying on reasoning and logical analysis to explore fundamental questions about existence, knowledge, ethics, and the nature of reality.

A lived Philosophy finds meaning from experience and appreciates awareness and recognition of the interlink between thoughts, words, and actions and how personal actions are reflected in the progress or chaos of society as the case may be.

Philosophy often deals with subjective experiences while Science expresses objective realities. These two realities need to form a unified experience, just as a common relationship between general relativity and quantum mechanics is necessary.

Unfortunately, philosophy and science have faced a grave dichotomy and have experienced an ever-greater gulf in our times. Philosophers cannot express scientific realities well enough while science has little clue about what goes on in Philosophy. Science started as a Philosophy, but while Philosophy has been unable to keep up with the advancement of science, scientists have been too busy with the advancement of science to have any concern with Philosophy.

Why should we care about Philosophy? Philosophy, being the study of the fundamental nature of reality, existence, and attitudes, acts as a guiding principle for behaviour. Philosophy gives us the right perspective on how we can navigate the many potholes of this life.

Without deepening our interest in Philosophy, it will be easy to disregard ethics. Without an ethical approach, no matter the degree of advancement in science, humanity is set for doom.

Ethics creates a balance that prevents the pot of scientific advancement to spill, and it is through an in-depth Philosophy that this can be developed.

I have come across many Philosophers who have little interest in science and are very biased toward it. Also, I have met many scientists who have already concluded that what cannot be shown objectively does not have any intrinsic meaning.

Subjective intuitions and thoughts may have a high degree of variance, but it is in the attested experience of this that we have a leap of faith into the next phase of reality which expands ad infinitum.

We, once more have to discover the point of coagulation between the narrative of subjective philosophy and objective science. A close symmetry between mind and matter is necessary for maximising the potential of this stage of the journey.

What we disregard, that which we think is unnecessary and ignore, may constitute the answer and may be the clue to our escape and progress. This bias described above, between the subjective and the objective, which can be the clue to our freedom, may be related to the tale of a girl and the spider woman.

The Girl and the Spider Woman

Many years ago, a little girl was playing in the woods when she saw a trail of smoke emerging from a hole in the ground. She peered down and saw the Spider Woman weaving through the loom; she began to teach the little girl how to weave.

The little girl watched with amazement as the Spider Woman hand flitted rhythmically backward and forwards across the loom, forming complex patterns of light and colour, going round and round like the stars and the planets as if she were bringing the very world into existence with form and colour and harmony and secrete meaning.

Principle 13: BECOMING – Itakun

A cosmic web was being woven into existence in which every part was related to every other part, and all centring on a hole in the middle of the cloth

"Always leave a hole in the middle of the blanket, my dear, won't you?" warned the Spider Woman, *"Like spiders always do. Otherwise, you may get caught in your own web!"*

That is the link between scientific objectivism and philosophical idealism. A focus only on one aspect with disregard to the other may get us caught in the web without any means of escape.

We have to leave *'a hole in the middle of the blanket'*. That reserved hole will be central to our escape. Our freedom lies where we would rather not look. It is dangerous to be biased and opinionated.

Objectivism and subjectivism need each other to survive, just as the body, brain and soul must work together to stay awake.

Between What and Why?

The effort towards finding a relationship between scientific equations and life experiences is ultimately a quest for the connection between 'what' and 'why'.

The great responsibility of our age, if we are to discover in full this reality and interconnectedness of everything, is to bridge the gap between philosophy and science. I believe science will find its ultimate purpose when it embraces true philosophy. Real philosophy must also make effort towards embracing the prodigality of science, where science, in turn, becomes for her, a parable for healing, clarifying, explaining, and authenticating the many ambiguities surrounding her studies.

This point of arrival between ethical philosophy and natural philosophy, in which science will be the very discovery of the reality and supreme potency of a real existential *'Theory of Everything'* is from where we will see the interconnectedness of everything and the realization of reality itself as an existential continuum.

I shall further describe this quest of mastering our interconnectedness by looking at three of the classical theories which has informed the development of Western ideas: Leonardo da Vinci's Vitruvian Man, Freud's Psychoanalysis, and Dante's Divine Comedy.

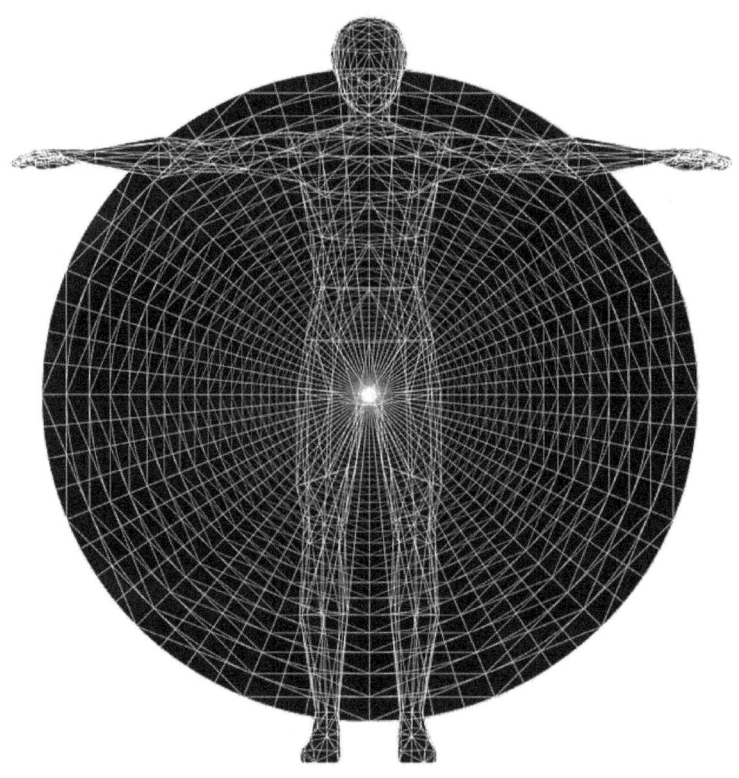

Vitruvian Man

Vitruvian Man and Itakun

Leonardo da Vinci was not just a painter. He was also a sculptor, writer, inventor, architect, engineer, mathematician and anatomist. He is indeed a literal depiction of a man at the centre of everything, which is expressed in one of his drawings: The Vitruvian Man.

The Vitruvian man, according to da Vinci, is an exploration of the theories about human proportions as set forth by the ancient Roman architect Vitruvius. Vitruvius believed that the human body was a microcosm of the universe and that the proportions of the body reflected the order and harmony of the natural world.

Leonardo da Vinci wrote of the Vitruvian man, *"Man has been called the world in miniature; and certainly, this name is well bestowed, because, inasmuch as man is composed of earth, water, air, and fire, his body resembles that of the earth."*

Leonardo da Vinci saw the Vitruvian Man as a representation of the ideal human form, based on the principles of proportion and harmony that govern the natural world. The drawing has become a symbol of the intersection between art and science, and the realisation of ourselves as part of and link between others.

Freud's Psychoanalysis

Sigmund Freud is regarded as the Father of Psychoanalysis. He developed the psychoanalytic theory of personality development, which argued that personality is formed through conflicts among three fundamental structures of the human mind: the id, the superego, and the ego.

The id is the primitive set of uncoordinated instinctual parts of the personality which is driven by the pleasure principle, seeking immediate gratification of basic needs and desires.

The superego is part of the personality that represents our moral values and ideals, it plays a critical role in our lives, acting as a conscience of the mind.

The ego is the organized, realistic, rational, and conscious part of the personality that mediates between the desires of the id and superego, attempting to satisfy both.

Freud also used the analogy of an iceberg to describe his psychoanalytic theory of the three levels of the mind: the conscious mind, the preconscious mind and the unconscious mind.

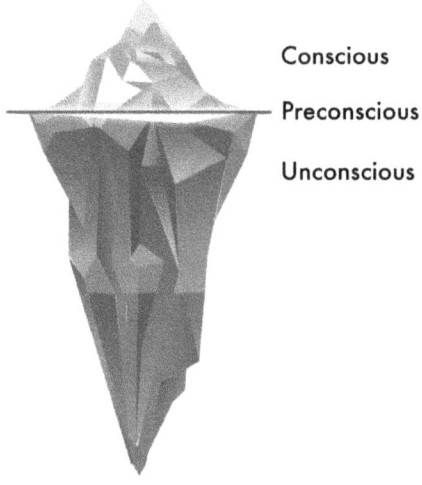

The Iceberg of Consciousness

The conscious mind is the tip of the iceberg, representing the thoughts, feelings, and perceptions that we are aware of in our everyday lives. This level of the mind includes our current thoughts, memories, and sensations, and is part of the mind that we can access and control.

The preconscious mind is the part of the mind just below the surface, representing our thoughts and memories that are not currently in our awareness but can be easily retrieved with some effort.

The unconscious mind is the largest and deepest part of the iceberg, representing thoughts, feelings, and memories that are outside of our conscious awareness. These thoughts and feelings are often hidden from us and may be difficult to access directly. However, they still influence our behaviour and emotional responses without us realising it.

Freud's psychoanalytic theory suggests that the unconscious mind plays a powerful role in shaping our thoughts, emotions, and behaviour, and that exploring the hidden aspects of our psyche can lead to greater self-awareness and personal growth.

Our thoughts are the focus of our present attention, but as Freud describes, what we are aware of from our thoughts is only the tip of the iceberg as compared to what we cannot. The goal of Freudian psychoanalysis is to make this unconscious reality conscious.

The id, ego, and superego are the constituents, while the conscious, preconscious, and unconscious are the levels of the mind. While they are not exactly the same, they can help us see how individual personalities interact with mind development and awareness toward forming a holistic person. We are the centre of the play between our minds and personalities.

Dante's Divine Comedy

Dante is considered the greatest Italian poet, best known for The Divine Comedy, an epic poem which is one of the world's most important works of literature.

The poem, which is divided into three sections, follows a man, generally assumed to be Dante himself, as he travels, first through Hell (inferno), then into Purgatory (Purgatorio), and his eventual liberating journey into Heaven (Paradiso),

In Inferno, Dante describes his descent through the nine circles of Hell, guided by the Roman poet Virgil. Each circle represents a different sin and punishment, with the worst being reserved for traitors, who are frozen in a lake of ice.

In Purgatorio, Dante ascends the seven levels of Mount Purgatory, where souls are purged of their sins before entering Heaven and Dante meets many souls who are working to expiate their sins, including his beloved Beatrice, who serves as his guide through the final part of the journey.

In Paradiso, Dante ascends through the nine celestial spheres of Heaven, guided by Beatrice and other saints and angels. Each sphere represents a different virtue, and Dante meets various historical and mythological figures.

Merging Dante, Freud and Leonardo

We may ask what the utilities of these three studies are in the Journey Forward toward becoming and in relation to Itakun.

Let us first make a comparison between Dante and Freud: Dante's Divine Comedy is an echo of Freud's Psychoanalytical description of the id, ego, and superego, but in an experiential way.

Inferno, the first part of the Divine Comedy, can be seen as a journey through the human psyche's shadow called Id, which contains all of the repressed, unconscious desires and impulses deemed unacceptable. Dante's journey through the circles of Hell can be seen as a descent into the shadow, where he encounters the various punishments of the souls who have committed sins.

Purgatorio can be seen as a journey through the psyche's ego (speaking of Freud) and can be seen as a process of purification and transformation, where we confront our insufficiencies and work to overcome them.

Paradiso relates to Freud's superego which is part of the psyche that internalises moral and ethical standards. Dante's ascent to Paradiso can be seen as a process of enlightenment and self-actualisation.

Principle 13: BECOMING – Itakun

Overall, the Divine Comedy adventure can be seen as a journey of individuation, where Dante confronts the various aspects of his own psyche and works to integrate them into a whole. Through his journey, he gains a deeper understanding of himself and the world around him, ultimately achieving a state of transcendence.

Dante's Journey bears relevance with the Journey we have made so far in order to bloom through chaotic times, having journeyed from the chaos of the Journey Back now unto the becoming stage of the Journey Forth.

We must imagine the trilogy of Dante's journey happening simultaneously. This is of course how the Journey Back and the Journey Forward is. We are the theatre of hell, purgatory, and paradise. The mission is to remove the inferno with a proper attitude and planning against chaos, to shorten Purgatorio through a necessary attitude to the Journey Back, and lengthen our Paradiso, by developing an attitude and mindset towards becoming the best version of ourselves through the necessary healing process of becoming.

This process of healing was termed Individuation by Swiss psychiatrist Carl Jung. Individuation is a psychological concept which refers to the process of integrating the various aspects of one's personality and involves facing and resolving conflicts and contradictions within oneself into a harmonious whole in order to become a unique and whole individual.

Individuation is an experience which involves the development of the ego, the conscious self, and the integration of the unconscious, which includes the personal and collective unconscious.

This process requires confronting and resolving inner conflicts, such as the tension between the ego and the self, as well as integrating various archetypes that represent different aspects of the psyche, which enables the individual to arrive at the self, which is the centre of the psyche and represents the totality of the individual, both conscious and unconscious.

A becoming is not just beneficial to us as individuals, but equally advantageous for our progeny. We are a bundle of gene cells: DNA dating back to our most ancient ancestors and inside of us is a multitude of living entities waiting for our consistency in order to be free, which in turn will be propagated to our children.

Life, in truth is a symbiosis between the past and present, between the seen and unseen, between the mind and matter, between the conscious and the unconscious.

Man, with the right belief, mindset, and discipline, is capable of realising himself within the past, the present, and the future, which is represented in his attitudes and perception, within his will, intellect, and memory.

Now, having analysed Dante and Freud, let us see, in what light they reflect Leonardo da Vinci.

Once we accept ourselves, together with our ignorance and moral insufficiencies, with the proper realistic attitude towards working towards becoming the best version of ourselves, we are then the Vitruvian Man.

As Leonardo da Vinci's Vitruvian Man illustrates, man becomes the link between everything, and everything is linked with him. Man is the centre of everything but he always exists as a dependent. Man can be aware through the experience of such Journeys described, of how every factor of the universe is joined together within his centrifuge.

It is important, as with da Vinci, Freud, and Dante, to discover the potential in the internal, external, and experiential self, merging the past and future, as now.

Principle 13: BECOMING – Itakun

This is the philosopher's joy, one filled with this knowledge and experience, who delights in simply watching this interconnectedness and marvels at his importance and centrality in existence.

We have the potential to bring to conscious awareness the many subconscious paths at play within us to be revealed and healed, the goal gets lighter by widening the liberating experiences of the Journey Forward and reducing the depth of negativity in the Journey Back.

Just as with the Vitruvian Man as the centre of his external surroundings, Freudian analysis shows the internal dimension of our state too, which transcends simply what we think we can control, but which goes so deep into the vast area of which we cannot control. Yet, we are a multitude of all these, a constituent of everything ancient and modern.

What is important is to realise that we are the centre, the theatre, and arena of varied forces at play, both internal and external. If we gatecrash our way unto this stage, the internal or external forces will usurp the control over us. When we take the Journey Back and the Journey Forward as a process towards arriving at this stage, we help ourselves, and even those whom we are unaware of align with the reality of existence and liberation.

It is our responsibility to coordinate and discipline these forces in such ways where we are able to continue this Journey Forward and not to dive back within the realms where we struggle unnecessarily. This grand interconnectivity of everything as us is what Itakun is about. We are the Itakun.

The Risk of Presumption

The realization of ourselves as Itakun and a humble discipline and responsibility is a step to self-actualisation. A realisation which is at the same time a glory and a responsibility, liberating and overwhelming.

Man can realise himself to be the centre of 'everything', towards liberation or towards perdition. The danger exists when we attain this point without following the Journey process. We face a real psychological dilemma and potential psychotic breakdown.

We cannot jump the gun, reality would resist this. This reality can be a responsibility when we realise our incompetence in the face of reality. We can hardly handle the truth when we jump the gun. If we hop on this awareness without following the journey we may become overwhelmed by the responsibility, and this can result in mental illness.

If we have truly made this journey, we shall be maintaining this realisation with calm, peaceful, and humble wariness without apathy. A keen awareness of becoming is based, not on prowess, but as a matter of the benevolence of reality.

By experiencing the Journey Forward described thus far, man experiences an existential reality where the entire cosmological macrocosm is in tune with the microcosm of his nature. It reveals an existence in which everything is perfectly proportioned, where there is a harmony of dynamics and balance of known and unknown as a reference to him and the possibilities and potential he holds.

This is indeed very liberating. Glorious is the calm realisation and recognition of our importance and necessity in the grand scheme of things, and the entire universe is conspiring in our favour.

I said the best description of Itakun to the best of my knowledge is matrix, but there is no better explanation towards this process and aspect to make than the Matrix movie itself.

Principle 13: BECOMING – Itakun

Carl Jung was reputed to say *"The world will ask you who you are, and if you don't know, the world will tell you"*.

This is what happened in The Matrix where there is a struggle between Neo and the sentinels about the realisation of either man or the System as 'The Matrix'. If we do not realise this, we will fall to the whims and caprices of the dictates of the System. If we realise this, with calm and ease, no System will have any power over us.

The Matrix Movie

The Matrix is a science fiction movie where machines created the Matrix — a massive simulation of the Earth— to keep humanity under their control and available as a power source.

These machines have created a new generation of people, fully integrated into the 'Matrix' and reared in womb-like pods, from whom they could harvest energy.

Outside this Matrix, the last dregs of humanity were forced deep below the surface of the Earth, where they built a massive city called Zion. Some citizens of Zion believe in the Prophecy of The One — a quasi-religious doctrine that predicts that humanity's original leader will be reborn inside the Matrix.

This chosen one will be capable of reshaping the simulation, freeing the humans enslaved by the Machines, and bringing peace to Earth.

One of these true believers is Morpheus who begins to suspect that Thomas Anderson, a hacker who calls himself "Neo", could be The One.

There followed a series of efforts to awaken Neo and make him discover and act on a life given mission of rescuing humanity. The encounter between Trinity, one of Morpheus' crew, with Neo and their eventual love affairs was the high point of the movie where this realisation of love ultimately rescued Zion, though they both died in the process.

Twenty years after the Matrix trilogy, a sequel was released. In this movie, titled Matrix Resurrection, Neo was seen inside the Matrix and unaware of his past, he lives as a very successful video game designer.

Thomas Anderson, as he is called, designs 'The Matrix' series of video games, based on his vague memories as Neo. Thomas bases the character of Trinity on Tiffany, a woman he meets in a coffee shop who like him has no recollection of her past exploits.

He went through a series of mental breakdowns which necessitated a regular appointment with a psychiatrist who tries to talk him through his experiences stating they are an illusion. He is offered a blue pill to calm his breakdowns. Once more he encounters Morpheus who reintroduces a red pill and is torn between the choice of taking the red pill and the blue pill.

He opted for the red pill which again led him down the rabbit hole of self-consciousness and self-awareness and its associated discipline. This then culminated in his work towards Tiffany's rediscovery of herself as Trinity and her eventual rescue from The Matrix.

Link Between the Matrix Movie and Matrix as Itakun

What is the connection between Thomas Anderson (Neo) the game developer in The Matrix Resurrection and the 'iceberg' in Freud's psychological work of bringing the subconscious and unconscious in line with a self-discovery?

Thomas' mental breakdown came to be regarded by the psychiatrist as a purely psychological ailment where he continued

Principle 13: BECOMING – Itakun

to consume the blue pill. The blue pill is a method of perception, effective, perhaps at certain path of the Journey, but not at this point as he dived from the conscious to the subconscious. The objective to the subjective.

Realisation of 'The Matrix' is not an elimination of the material. It is an integration of matter and mind, the subconscious and the conscious as epitomised by you. You are the link, the *Itakun to s'ogba, t'o s'agbe, t'o s'elegede.*

The future, I believe, would be rife with this subject of balancing the mental and spiritual with the emotional and psychological. The journey of self-discovery is a personal one, Morpheus once said to Neo: *"Unfortunately, no one can be told what the Matrix is. You have to see it for yourself."*

There is a certain attractiveness of this position for the person who has followed this Journey thus far which does not stop until they have taken the 'red pill' of a disciplined journey of self-discovery, not out of compulsion, but because of an innate motivation to do so.

In this book (the red pill), you have discovered a means to deepen and widen your purpose and irrespective of what the system dictates, you will not be restful until you fulfil your purpose.

The world will ask you who you are, and if you don't know, the world will tell you – and this will not necessarily be according to what you desire or of your freedom as a primary motive, but upon the idiosyncrasies of the world.

Those who have gained this experience are no more at the mercy of the System, even if they work in and with the System.

At the core of The Matrix movie, is the realisation of love, as the powerful force and energy employed for the deconstruction of the

Matrix. Neo would not have had the motivation to rescue Trinity out from the Matrix without love.

Without love, it is next to impossible to move on with purpose. This is because it is not just our awareness that creates our becoming, what really fosters this stage is our desire, passion and action: because real love signifies action, it is a verb. It is love which is the actual energy of the cosmos, not money.

The passion at which we follow this love is what makes us self-actualise. But, the nature of love once more has to be rediscovered in our times. Without love, we cannot become. Love pulses our ability for forward momentum. If we do not love, we shall not only stall but actually regress!

Between Purpose and Passion

Leonardo da Vinci once said: *"I awoke only to find that the rest of the world was still asleep."* Like Morpheus, once awake, we become inclined to search for the many 'Ones' who litter all humanity and desire to see them wake up.

Our awakening impels us to share what we know, and there also is no room for the desire for superiority because we realize how absolutely helpless our efforts towards arriving this creates.

Henceforth, our desire will be geared towards waking up the sleeping giant in ourselves and others, no more as a show of superiority, but rather a motive strengthened by a legacy through sharing. The highest form of giving is in communicating reality to others through action.

When the fabric of world events aligns itself with your prosperity and causes a shift in your favour, you are able to integrate the past and the future within the present, without distress or anxiety. This influence is built more in actions than words. Words are

Principle 13: BECOMING – Itakun

cheap, what is needed is love and compassion. This harks back to the utilisation of leadership for service and peace.

The Itakun person takes cues and energy from the past. They know current events in the world are directed from hidden icebergs (past events) and as such they employ memory, which becomes for them, not just memory but reality. They realise the deception of time and that the past is only energy for the future and can become a confluence in himself as a presence.

The Itakun person is passionate for truth and rejects the temptation of condemning memory to the past and derives a great forge towards positivity.

The Itakun person is acutely aware of how falsehood ends in nihilism, and as such they reject anything false. Only truth matters and it sustains the journey.

When an Itakun person becomes committed to memory and the subconscious, they become their thoughts and utilise legacy to arrive at crafting a parable for reality.

- ◉ They realise they have a continual duty to repair the present from the past. They realise, without being overwhelmed, that the entire origin of the universe and of history is under their obligation.
- ◉ They see a commonality pattern, a dimension of habits, and plans which can be iterated to success. They understand how their experiences, practices and work can be gradually scaled from a lower experience to a higher plane. They realise their importance in the face of history.
- ◉ They understand the Journey Back as having a great utility to break the slavery of an unrecognised iceberg of the subconscious and bring it to the liberating light of the consciousness.

By Journeying Forward you repair the past and in repairing the past (Journeying Back) you develop a greater capacity for transforming your Journey Back into a Journey Forward.

The Itakun person spends their entire life weaving this legacy into reality. They temporarily become the protagonist of reality, the centre, the leader, before becoming history as they let go.

A society is a reflection of the legacy created from the stories of its past ancestors. Ancestors are legacies because everyone has crafted a story true or false, lasting or ephemeral, and it is this Legacy which the Itakun person spends his entire life weaving according to reality. He is the real protagonist of history.

What is the point of being the centre of everything? Why should anyone care for this awareness? It is in order to a personal story that is aligned with reality.

This we shall explain further in the next Principle - A Parable for Living.

Practical Suggestions to Become Itakun

1. What interlinked experience of yours can you remember which has really impacted your awareness of the great truth of life?
2. Who, and what things are you most connected with, from which you can draw life and gusto?
3. Are you confident and comfortable under your skin? If not, what work will you do to become so?

PRINCIPLE 14. BECOMING - PARABLE FOR LIVING

Live Reality Intensely.

Luigi Giussani

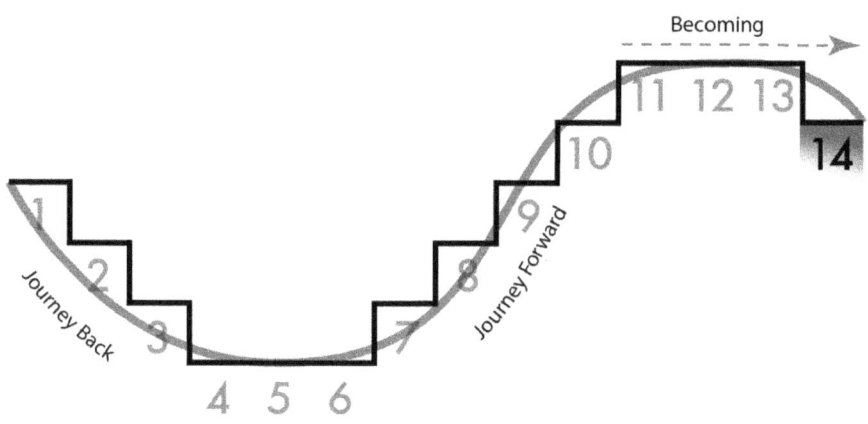

Principle 14

Principle 14: BECOMING – Parable for Living

Can there be anything which truly endures; and is able to defy entropy and gravity? Something which would be a bridge between the physical and the metaphysical and yet be real? What then is the consequence of being, in the face of everything integrated as you?

The first reaction of anyone confronted with a responsibility described in the previous chapter is one of being overwhelmed. Who wants any added trouble amidst the complexity which already exists in the world and in our lives?

But the point is, if we have made it up here as part of a process, we already have a strong sense of purpose and a capacity matching the responsibility to embark on a mission beyond ourselves.

Here, we can begin to see life in its simplicity and to understand that whatever complexity or evil we experience in the world is borne, not so much of the System or of creation, but principally out of the inability to conquer ourselves.

One who has conquered himself may be able to have a positive perspective, even in the face of evil, such as the story of the madman narrated below.

The Madman and the Scorpion

There was once a man who was known as "the madman" in his village. Despite this label, he was always peaceful and content.

People asked him, *"Why are you always so calm? Don't you worry about anything?"*

The madman replied, *"Why should I worry? It doesn't change anything. If something is going to happen, it will happen whether I worry about it or not. So why bother?"*

One day, the madman was walking by a river and saw a scorpion struggling in the water. Without hesitation, he reached in and pulled the scorpion to safety. However, as he did so, the scorpion stung him.

The madman didn't panic or get angry. He simply said to himself, *"Ah, the nature of the scorpion is to sting."*

A bystander who had witnessed the event asked the madman, *"Why did you save the scorpion if you knew it would sting you?"*

The madman replied, *"Why should the scorpion's nature change mine? My nature is to help others, even if it means risking harm to myself."*

The Power in Perspectives

The perspective which we live our story matters. Just as the "madman", we may be unable to change the narrative, but we can change the perspective of the narrative. A glass of water half-way can either be looked at as half-empty, or half-full.

One may live in a glass house with fine linens and still see life as a tragedy, and another person may dwell under a thatched roof and create a narrative as the happiest person on earth.

The "madman" understands because he has already conquered himself to the extent that, not only is he able to freely demonstrate compassion but he also realises that worrying does not change anything and that it is possible to live a peaceful and contented life by accepting things as they are.

This is what happens when we get through this state as a process and experience, not as something thrust or imposed on us.

But we may ask, won't the attitude of the "madman" simply allow the arrogant and outspoken to have their way all the time. Wouldn't it be wrong to remain silent in the face of errors and advocate appeasement?

There are two questions we may use to solve this:

1. What is the reason? and,
2. What is the lesson behind an action?

Reason and lesson.

We seek to understand. For instance, the madman may ask, why did the scorpion sting? 'Oh, it is in the nature of scorpions to sting'.

But what makes it part of their nature? Scorpions are typically nocturnal and tend to avoid confrontations, but in order to survive, evolution has genetically transformed them to sting as a form of self-defence or to capture prey.

And the madman may ask 'What is the lesson behind the scorpion stinging?'. 'Oh, my action was perceived as a further provocation against the scorpion's predicaments'.

Because the "madman" understands from the point of perspective and is able to approach a seemingly unfair reality from the rationale of peace and equanimity, he would be better placed to maintain the peace of his domain.

The point of perspective and how it favours the one who journeys and eventually affects the brash and evil, can be better explained from the African Story of Alero and Serving Plate.

Blooming Through Chaotic Times

Alero and the Serving Plate

Once upon a time, a man had two wives, Awa and Alero. Awa continually maltreated Alero and for whatever reason, their husband turned a blind eye. Awa was wealthy and Alero lived in penury, yet they were both living under the same roof.

In those days, everything was washed in the river; dishes, clothes and self. Alero took the dirty household utensils to wash by the river and as she was doing this, a small serving plate which belonged to Awa fell into the river and was swept away by the river.

Principle 14: BECOMING – Parable for Living

Alero, knowing Awa, would not accept any of her stuff missing, summoned courage and told Awa about this incident. As expected, Awa would have nothing of it and she would also not accept a replacement plate: she wanted the original one washed away by the river.

Alero's Journey Back

Alero had no choice but to follow the deep river course, wailing and lamenting about a seemingly forlorn attempt to find her colleague's serving plate because she knew it would be suicidal to attempt to wade into the deep river.

In the process of looking for the serving plate, she wandered deep into the jungle down the river course into the deep forest.

Now, not only was she unable to find the serving plate, but she also lost the route back home.

Deep into the night, Alero was weeping when a man appeared to her. The man asked her what was wrong and she narrated her ordeals. Not only would she dare go home without finding Awa's serving plate, but, even if she ran away (as she was considering) she was now lost in the thick jungle and susceptible to being killed and eaten by wild animals.

The man pointed to a little path nearby and told Alero to go deeper, where she would find two types of oranges: ripe and unripe.

"Do not pick the oranges which are ripe," he said, "pick only three of the oranges which are unripe. Break the first fruit and follow the path of your gumption, this will lead you back to your route. Break another when you are at the front of your house, and when you get inside, lock the door before you break the last."

The man journeyed on and Alero was again by herself. She walked through the path and immediately discovered just by the side of the road the beautiful ripen oranges with short trees. As she was hungry, she felt tempted to pluck but did not and was determined to keep to the promise she made to the man.

On the other side, she saw unripened oranges, right into a thick, thorny bush; though her body was torn by the forest thorns which turned her body bloody, though she was stung by insects in the process and though she was terrified by snakes and scorpions, she was determined to get the fruit. She climbed onto a tall orange tree, where she plucked three hardened, non-edible green oranges.

Alero's Journey Forward

When she got down from the tree, Alero broke the first fruit. Hungry and worn out, she followed her gumption and discovered her way home. It was dawn by the time she got home.

When she got to the house door, she broke the second orange and behold, many livestock appeared, more than 500 sheep, goats, fowls, and turkey, the nature of which, based on the age she was living, would make her wealthy forever.

As if this was not enough, she entered the house, went straight into her room and bolted the door. Then she broke the third orange; at once the room was overflowing with money and jewels, together with Awa's lost serving plate. She was stunned.

The following day, Alero narrated her story to her husband and Awa. She gratefully gave Awa back her serving plate and also divided everything she got into 3 equal parts. One for her, one for her husband and one for Awa, her colleague wife who had once maltreated her.

Awa would not have any of this. She took back her serving plate and decided to make a similar adventure of her own.

Awa the Copy-Cat

At mid-morning, she went to the river bank, threw her serving plate into the river and followed the river course into the thick jungle.

She met the same man with whom she narrated her plight.

The man pointed to a similar forest path nearby and told Awa she was going to find two different types of oranges; she too should pluck three of the unripe oranges and should not venture near those which were ripe.

He also gave similar injunctions about how she should break the first fruit and follow the path of her gumption which would lead her back to her route, and how she should also break the other fruits when she gets home and locked in her room.

The man journeyed on and when Awa was by herself, she walked through the path and when she discovered the short tree, with beautiful ripened oranges by the side of the road, she couldn't be bothered anymore.

She began to ruminate on how Alero must have told her a lie. She immediately opined that beautiful proximal ripen fruits should be better than hidden dark green fruits.

When she got to the tree, she immediately plucked close to 20 oranges as she believed the more she was able to grasp, the wealthier she would become. She saw the oranges succulent and fresh and as such, she immediately broke one to eat.

Immediately, crawling reptiles ventured from everywhere across the forest and ran after her, she was bitten by snakes and stung by scorpions in her panic. She said to herself, '*this must be the same ordeal Alero must have passed through before hitting the jackpot*' so she broke the second orange.

At this, wild animals came by and tore her to pieces. The following day, while the hunters were returning home from their spree, they found the dead body of Awa on the road almost unrecognisable because she was torn to pieces by wild animals.

One moral of the story is: You have to craft your own story and not be a copycat. You have to craft your story in line with the benevolent truth of the universe. And, as related between the case of Awa and Alero, we see how knowledge is necessary, but an understanding of the reason behind the knowledge is what really prevails. You have to follow the right perspective.

Paradox and Perspective

From this we enter into the utility of perspectives in crafting ones freedom or one's ruin, as was the case between Alero and Awa's story.

In order to make comparisons between perspectives, let us enter once more into the study of physical phenomena, here, we can understand how scientists may arrive at the conclusion of the black hole phenomena- a regional space where all information and experience is lost as the nihilistic end and conclusion of everything. But, in our times, many scientists are beginning to discover pieces of evidence which suggest that this very black hole, where all the physical laws seem to collapse, may actually be the beginning of the Big Bang where everything begins.

Principle 14: BECOMING – Parable for Living

In the same light, many have observed the change and decay which the Law of Entropy introduces and have concluded this enforced energy usurpation is a result of the tyranny of nature, of which we are incapable and powerless at remedying.

Whereas, others have seen the same entropy phenomena as spontaneous creativity of heat and time giving humanity a chance to enact positivity into the grand scheme of existence. It is a question of perspective.

To help us in acquiring the right perspective in order to move forward and reach fulfilment, I introduce the logos rationale.

Logos

Logos (or universal life force) relates to reason, order, communication, logic, rationality, and the analytical principles which underlie the universe and human thought. There is a close connection between how we think, what we say, the stories we craft, and the legacy we live in history, in relation to reality.

Let us first look at reason from the perspective of thought. How does thought begin?

From a scientific perspective, we may say thoughts are a complex iteration between the neurons of our brain. Our brain, which is the primal substance of our thoughts, teems with information accumulated from our experiences. This information is exchanged and continually elaborated on and weaved into a web of experiences which become stories. It is this story which becomes history and is passed on as information to progeny.

Thoughts, words, stories, and information are the make of Logos, which eventually forge our future. It is logos which sieves history towards the conception of reality, for, stories build or decay in proportion to their alignment with reality. Logos is the intrinsic order of creation, which has an order through which we can make an experiential discovery of the underlying reality of the nature of our existence.

On the bedrock of logos the entire chemistry of the universe is created and sustained because of its relation to reality. In Principle 12, I borrowed a definition of reality by Swami Bhaktivedanta as an existence that cannot be vanquished.

So, how does this add on? We live in an increasingly schizophrenic age where rules and policies keep changing. Perceived virtuous actions yesterday have become criminal today and behaviours considered yesterday as criminal are now judged as most virtuous, and in the process, we have this entire culture of cancelling and blaming.

I often make a funny scenario of this cultural confusion from how undecided and diverse dietary experts can be when differentiating healthy from unhealthy meals.

Something is real to the extent which it is able to withstand and sustain itself amidst every other factor, and able to maintain a malleable capability to adapt to changing circumstances.

The case of the "madman" as narrated previously, is of one who has stepped outside the boundary of this relativistic experience towards an acceptance of the nature of realities and yet is himself unaffected by the whims and caprices of his environment. This is because he has an adaptable perspective which utilises reason to arrive at lessons against which his position with reality is tested. To reason, you have to be able to think.

To reason, you have to be able to think and thinking is integral to existing, as Rene Descartes, the French Philosopher would observe when he said *"I think, therefore I am"*.

Principle 14: BECOMING – Parable for Living

We Become Stories

In practical analysis, we may say thoughts are born of beliefs which reflect the words we speak and are translated into how we act. But, how shall we test this against reality?

Jean Piaget, considers that the process of thinking and intellectual development could be regarded as an extension of the biological process born from our evolutionary adaptation.

In this regard, we can say, any living organism is a constituent of information from the DNA and as such an individual is a complex, tightly integrated story composed of different informational processes.

The information is not simply mental or subjective. Organisms and matter, are a combination of different information and processes which form a bunch of stories constituted into history.

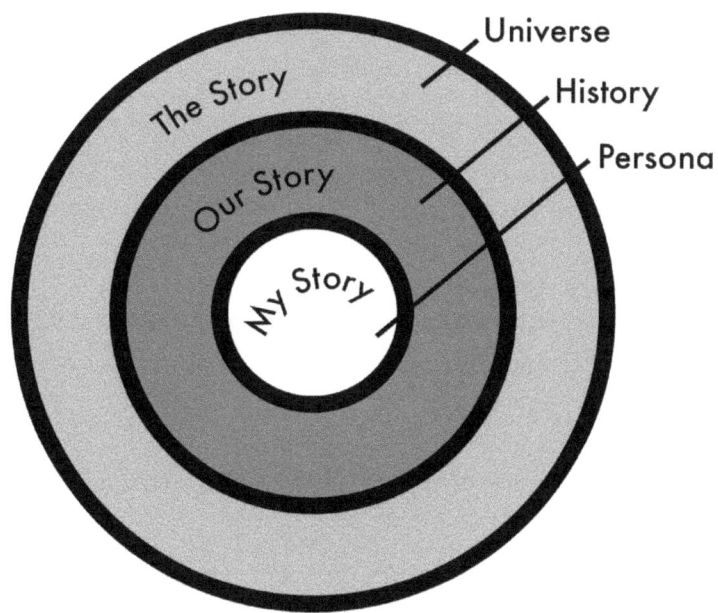

We Become Stories

How we are Constituents of Information

We find this interconnectedness of information in everything, and often time, we don't make the story; we have to align ourselves with it, and the more our story is aligned to reality, the more it can resist any idiosyncrasy encountered.

Sometimes, events take place which are beyond our comprehension, but in so far as we can reason, apply, test and judge them in line with truth, we may arrive at a lasting phase where how we live can positively influence our society and in fact, the global and universal order of life. My story can be in line with our story and in tune with the reality of the universe.

Crafting Our Stories

We acquire a fruitful correspondence in proportion to how we craft our story relative to Reality. This is how we can discover the ultimate use of story in creating a perpetual dimension of charting something transcendental.

As Jung says, *"Everybody acts out a myth, but very few people know what their myth is. And you should know what your myth is because it might be a tragedy and maybe you don't want it to be."*

Our thoughts, words and actions become a sustainable web of stories and experiences happening through the accumulated factor of logos.

It is our responsibility to make stories out of our myths and use our 'logos' to align with the reality of the cosmos in accordance with the perspective of perpetual positivity of the nature of existence: to build an experience out of our stories, and to make this experience correspond to a reality which cannot be vanquished.

Principle 14: BECOMING – Parable for Living

Victor Frankl, the Austrian Psychotherapist, said, *"Any story not commensurate with truth and reality will be condemned to non-being."*

The goal which is worthy of striving after is to align ourselves with what contributes positively to our personal development, the cultural progress of society, and global cohesion in proportion to the truth of our conscience and discern a right perspective to the revealed realities of the universe.

The progress of a society is rooted in the belief in a common story that exist in people's imagination, such as that which you are presently crafting through your daily life experiences. Your domain will ultimately survive relative to the correspondence of your life to reality. You matter in the grand cosmic web of reality.

We should do our best to enter a narrative which transcends ourselves, our family, and our nation, but from where we can even discover ourselves as the most meaningful factor in the positive working of the entire cosmos. Daunting, but true.

A player of reality is able to discover himself in the great truths of history and he is not simply a passive observer, but he bears a resemblance to history and nature. He creates his own unique story in synergy, and as a bonus, to the grand story of life!

By the application of the Principles in this book, by living experiences intensely and approaching life as a reality, naturally and in proper time, without necessarily embarking on anything 'spectacular', we can understand how history exists now, (a lived synergy) and how life is a positive movement of a cosmological dimension.

Our culture and the entire cosmic realities are made up of stories and we can utilize these stories in proportion with their alignment to reality and our capacity to create an interlink where our individual story, finds a synergy with our collective story, which in turn finds vibration with the reality of the universe.

If we live truthfully and valuably enough, we can bring dreams into reality, vision unto actuality. We can find ourselves crafting and living a non-abstractive story which is full of meaning and which becomes a driving gusto for a meaningful existence.

We can experience the actions of the universe and align our own actions towards this great reality. We may ask, what is this action of the universe? The universe plays, it creates, it dances, it gives, it is continually in a relationship with its constituents as a singular story of a giving dimension. The universe is love telling you its story!

Nothing is realistically lost once one reaches this limit of the Journey Forward where we can discover the eternalness of our stories in the sands of time, and how this story is a synergy with our family, our nation, our world, and our entire existence. This is the parable for living!

How to Craft a Credible Story

We must craft a story proportional to the universal story on an incremental dimension, not just jumping to change the world.

We must continually test this universal proportion against a set of personal experiences and observe their veracity and capacity for success on a smaller scale before scaling up to a larger proportion.

Test what you can withstand and what you can do, right from the corner of your room. Big things are unnecessary, it is the consistency with which you craft your little tales in a realistic manner which matter.

The circumstances surrounding our lives when lived deeply, meaningfully, and realistically, are what would help us to be able to move out into reality and freedom.

Principle 14: BECOMING – Parable for Living

Every lesson in life's circumstances, everything which happens in the process of living, ultimately has a correspondence to our welfare according to the nature of our desires.

Repeatedly crafting lessons from reason, we can create our story using our experiences: where we perceive life ultimately as a comedy because there is a grand loving positivity to existence.

Here is the "madman's" perspective. Life is positive. *'Hakuna matata'*. Ultimately, everything is going to be all right.

The Grand Positivity of Experience

The goal of mastering both the Journey Back and Journey Forward is not towards creating something cyclic. Life is not cyclic, life is not static, and life is not retrogressive. Life may go back and forth but this cumulative experience has a positive dimension.

Life's purpose is to bloom and we can align ourselves with the grand positivity of existence by utilising the potential of the old to build the new such that at each repeated experience we continually bloom and add something positive to this great comedy.

As described in the introduction, history is a pendulum, but this pendulum does not swing from a static position. It moves forward, so your bet can only be on the Journey Forward, which is positive and optimistic. Even death (which we may see as a massive journey back) cannot deter the forward rhythm of life.

As we master the Journey Back, and bank this mastery unto a Forward perspective, we expand the potential for a positive outlook of life which reflects the non-dualism of everything and in synergy with the great positive cosmological story of existence.

Living our story authentically will bring about finding that transcendental intersection and tipping point at the tail end of the Journey Forward which brings about a forward momentum to the entire framework of the holistic journey.

We cannot start from bias. Reality encompasses everything and all perspectives!

The higher (or wider, when considering experience as spiral) we go, the easier it becomes. Not necessarily because life's situations get better or the journey is easier from an external perspective, but because we have developed the muscle to deal with them, not necessarily physically, but because we understand and are experienced.

From the multiplicity of our experiences, and each time we successfully progress from the Journey back unto the Journey Forward, we build a story which has the capacity to reduce the work of our transition and transformation.

The purpose of this non-dualistic positive rationalism of existence is to discover and find meaning and freedom in our state of becoming.

Here, we see the destination as every step of the journey with intense authenticity, and we experience leaps unto different levels of awareness where we discover the equanimity to accept the things we cannot change, acquire the courage to change the things we can, and derive the wisdom to know the difference.

But how and where does it end?

Infinity Now?

We have already discussed how the motive of our journey is to continually reduce the Journey Back and expand on the Journey Forward.

In the experience of this grand positivity of existence, can our Journey Back be completely absorbed into the Journey Forward?

Can the Journey Back be completely vanquished?

Principle 14: BECOMING – Parable for Living

- Can chaos be entirely done away with?
- Can we be in a satisfied comfortable and contented position perpetually?
- Can we derive strength and meaning from our insufficiencies?
- Can our consistency be seen as a destination rather than Journey?
- Can courage be without fear and confidence be without anxiety?
- Can memory be real and can the true past be touched as a presence?
- Can mothers perpetually birth something real and eternal?

It all boils down to the strength of our perspective. Now, let us return to the work of turning the present chaos into bloom by living life truthfully, courageously and intensely.

Practical Suggestions for the Parable of Living

1. What is life to you, what would make it meaningful? Write these ideas down.
2. Is your glass 'half full' or 'half empty'? Start looking for ways to see it half-full.
3. What would you live (or die) for?

AFTERWORD - THE PARABLE OF DADDY

"There is a time for everything and a season for every activity under the heavens"

Ecclesiastes 3:1

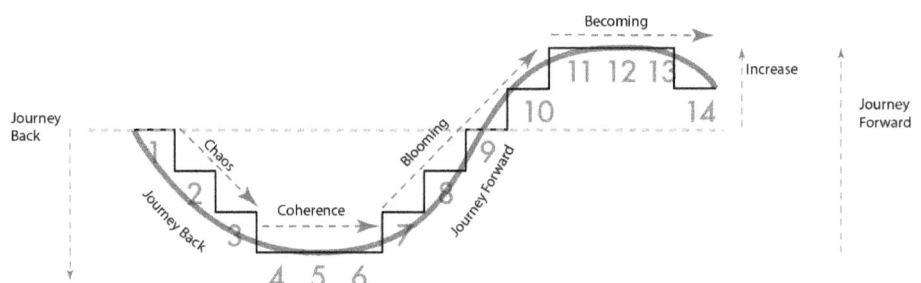

The 14 Principles Across Journey Back and Journey Forward

Afterword: Parable of Daddy

In 2011, when I suddenly lost my dad, I descended into such a dark, gory place (mentally) where it took enormous effort to love, forgive, and believe in goodness.

How drastically everything can change. The utter suddenness and senselessness of Daddy's demise and the circumstances leading to his death, deprived me of the ability to make any meaning out of reality. What remained of me then was fear, anger, intense sorrow and a deep anxiety about his state. I was utterly depressed and beaten.

I began to fully understand Macbeth's message in Shakespeare when he said; *'Life is a tale told by a fool, which is full of sound and fury.'* That is, we can descend into situations where everything becomes meaningless and nothing is within our grasp or under our control.

Sigmund Freud said, *"You haven't really become a man until you've gone through your father's death."* One knows the full depth of such a statement in proportion to one's love and devotion for one's father. Something of you goes forever with the passing of a loved one.

The emotions of those days presented me with two choices: give in to emotion by taking up a work of revenge (which is spontaneous and determinable); or float through the process of healing and hope for the future (which is slow and unsure).

I opted for the latter and took up the work, though making a conscious choice, but little knowing the route. It was a work which would entail looking where I would rather not look and going where I would rather not go, all within my emotions and through the circumstances of my daily actions. It was an experiential venture into a relational rabbit hole in order to verify the state of my dad's wellbeing. That was all I cared about.

I assumed the hypothesis that every obstacle faced in the course of my daily actions and family ordeals was the source of a wanting lesson and discovery of the fate of my dad. I just needed to know if he was alright wherever he was (whatever that means).

I began to hope and assume something bright would come out of my darkness and total mental breakdown. I was determined to confront all the maladies, bruises, and scourges surrounding my daily life with courage.

I would not take any circumstance of my life for granted. By consistently being true to my experiences, and owning them, I came to realise how every circumstance surrounding my life can be linked to my dad's, and how every choice I made has an infinite and universal dimension.

One of the deep experiences during those periods was my acute awareness of the thinness of the boundary between life here and beyond. I could very much have been the person who died, because I could almost grasp the 'multiversal' nature of existence. A similar awareness I experienced in the heart of the covid pandemic (a talk for another time).

The decision to venture for the welfare of my father, I knew, was a weird decision, so it wasn't something I could relate to anyone. I later discovered how common these thoughts and experiences are across many myths and great religious stories.

Jordan Peterson the Canadian Psychologist, for instance, pointed to the universality of such a quest which he identified with the adventure of *'Rescuing one's father from the belly of the fish'*, a term which he himself borrowed from the Pinocchio story.

The Story of Pinocchio

Pinocchio was a wooden puppet who was brought to life by a kind old man named Geppetto. One day, Geppetto went out to sea to fish and never returned. Pinocchio set out to find him and was told by a talking cricket that Geppetto had been swallowed by a giant fish.

Determined to rescue his father, Pinocchio dove into the ocean and swam to the fish. He climbed into the fish's belly and found Geppetto trapped inside. Pinocchio used his nose to tickle the fish until it sneezed and released them. Pinocchio and Geppetto were reunited and swam back to shore safely.

What I Discovered Under the Fish Belly

I Journeyed Back and I discovered how every ordeal, every life circumstance, and every lesson which happens for my progress in the process of living are links which correspond with the welfare of Daddy. I discovered that the process of 'rescuing my father from the belly of the fish', was actually a journey to finding myself and life's meaning.

Today I am most grateful, for I can see how life only seeks to plant itself in us through experience. An experience which is integrally linked, in a real sense, not only to my dad, but to my generation, to an entire plethora of ancient ancestors, to humanity, and to the entire cosmos. It is daunting, we are one!

I discovered, deep inside me, not simply my daddy, but that it is love which makes everything into unity. When you love and you care, you experience this synergy.

The loss of anything, money, job, or loved ones, is painful, and it can create a downward spiral which requires emotional, spiritual, mental, and psychological discipline to balance through and hold on.

By a patient and courageous living through (and not side-stepping) such experiences, you can cultivate your growth by maintaining a balanced awareness. While others are reaping early and creating further chaos, you are sowing through maturity in behaviour, which reaps a plenitude of rewards (which are not necessarily material) vaster than can be imagined.

Life is a Marathon Not a Sprint.

It is what we are unwilling to look at and where we are unprepared to go which gives a clue to what we seek and the necessity to realising reality. As Tom Peters says, *"Unless you walk out into the unknown, the odds of making a profound difference in your life are pretty low."*

By rescuing one's father from the belly of the fish, one becomes at peace with one's fate, and at the same time, heals one's trauma. It is a realisation which gives man enormous zest and gusto. No man can ever be the same after the realisation that he is not an island. We are all massively interconnected.

Life experience is the only initiation when lived intensely and experienced to its fullest. This is where freedom can be derived, and love is the prime mover of this positive adventure. For me, the Parable of Daddy is a personal experiential journey which became a transformation unto a Parable for Living.

Afterword: Parable of Daddy

Do you care for any of your departed, the more you miss them, the more your potential for happiness and peace. I also found an echo of this experience in Disney's 'The Lion King'.

The Lion King

In The Lion King, Simba's dead father, Mufasa's ghost appears to Simba and tells him that even though he is no longer physically present, his spirit will always be with him and guide him.

Mufasa encourages Simba to take back his rightful place as king and not let Scar rule. This brought about the song, *"He Lives In Me"*. Meaning that Mufasa's spirit is in Simba and he will always be with Simba, giving him the strength and guidance to fulfil his destiny as king. This concept of *"He Lives In Me"* suggests that the spirit of a deceased loved one continues to live on within those they left behind.

Stepping back a little from the spiritual meaning, genealogically, our fathers and ancestors' genes are always vibrating within us and it is our responsibility within the evolutionary framework to purify and make healthy these constituents by engaging in the work of being the best of ourselves.

It is a personal, internal journey. If this process is applied externally, as Hitler did, using eugenics in killing and maiming those unlike oneself, one misses the mark completely. This work is an internal one, by the application of Principles described in this book.

The Reward

If we search deep enough, we see how integrally linked the story of our departed loved ones are to our welfare. It is really not so much about them, but about us! We learn extensively from proper utilisation of memory.

When we love, we miss nothing. While grief may sometimes be the price of love, it is from here that we gain understanding, liberation, and peace, when we have the audacity to take up the journey. Everything calls, everything beckons. The worst opposition to realising this is ourselves when we become impatient and we don't pay attention. A piece of advice for the bereaved: Try to own your feelings and be true to yourself; mend any pending strife across the household; and don't treat the departed belongings as trash.

Making a Journey Back in order to bloom forward is about discipline and responsibility. This may entail facing the uncomfortable demons we meet in our relationships and in the execution of our daily duties under our individual circumstances.

This can be difficult, especially when we attempt this journey in solitude. It often requires companionship. This is what we try to do with people at ARC and You.

My Family

Dad left a complex family, out of a courageous adventure to work, balance and unify the seemingly impossible. He was a great leader.

It is no little work balancing the complexities of many constituents, especially in families. We often do more work in families, than in society. That is why many give up on families and turn instead to 'saving the world'. We tend to take the easier route and are impatient with those who would hold us back.

While I do not underestimate the work involved or oversimplify the complexity and sometimes the 'impossibility' of such venture, I have also discovered how innumerable it's returns are once mastered.

Afterword: Parable of Daddy

Dad never led from a comfortable space of the Journey Forward, he was often going through many Journey Back moments, but his vision of making his family work was unwavering.

We progress by a sincere service towards the peace of our domain, a lesson I discovered through the influence of my dad and the veracity of which I gained from experience.

This book is about human interdependency. When we better our lots, at an appropriate time, we will better our fate. Yes, there is a time for everything and a season for every activity under the heavens: But, I have discovered that, in all these:

- Birth trumps death
- Planting trumps uprooting
- Healing trumps killing
- Building trumps tearing down
- Laughing trumps weeping
- Dancing trumps mourning
- Gathering trumps scattering
- Embracing trumps aloofness
- Love trumps hate and
- Peace trumps war.

Sure, we can start from our own individual reality but the best means of tackling the fragility of life in my opinion is to be proactively and purposely prepared, and we can be sure to triumph and not fail if we bet on the grand positivity of experience and existence.

Blooming Through Chaotic Times

ACKNOWLEDGEMENTS

Evelyn, my wife. She is not just a wife; she is a friend and a mother. Thank you for supporting me in my Journeys Back and Forward.

Ifeoluwa, Mercy, and Maria my children. Writing this book is next to impossible without your moral support and understanding

To, Mrs. Olufunmilayo Ojo (Nee Ajayi-obe) (R.I.P), Mrs. Ronke Olloh, Canon Michael Branch, the effective fulcrums of my Journey Forward.

To Patrick, Peter-Paul, Helen, James, Mary, Stephen (R.I.P), Felicia, and Cecilia. For your great work in keeping the family intact in our Journeys Back and Forward.

To Ladey Adey, who has painstakingly proofread and edited this book, despite the personal journeys back and forth she's had to undergo in the process. For her numerous, advice, assistance, and invaluable mentorship.

Abbirose Adey who's helped with the book's illustration. She's a cat with nine lives! Her helpful advice, unbelievable professionalism, and disciplined work ethic have helped to see this book published to plan and standard.

Blooming Through Chaotic Times

REFERENCES

Always look back to your own experiences as a frame of reference.

Abbirose Adey

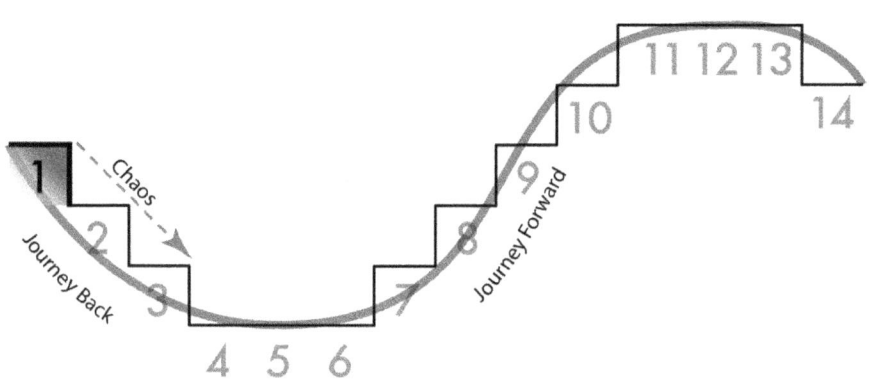

Principle 1

References

These books have highly influenced my thinking, my journey onto becoming and inspired me to write my book. They may help you on your Journey too.

Books

Anderson, Sandra et al, *Business The Ultimate Resource*, (A & C Publishers), 2006

Arp, Robert, *1001 Ideas*, (Octopus Books), 2013

Austin, David, *Managing Projects Large and Small*, (Havard Business School), 2004

Bhaktivedanta, Swami Prabhupada, *Beyond Birth and Death*, (The Bhaktivedanta Book Trust), 2018

Black, Jonathan, *The Sacred History*, (Quercus), 2014

Burg, Bob, & Mann, John David, *The Go-Giver*, (Penguin), 2015

Clarke, John, *Story of a Soul*, (ICS), 1996

Collodi, Carlo, *Pinocchio*, (Macmillan), 2017

Communion & Liberation Responsibles, *Memory: Method of the Event*, (Traces Booklets), 2006

Darwin, Charles, *The Origin of Species*, (Vintage), 2019

De Mello, Anthony, *Awareness*, (Zondervan), 1990

Dispenza, Joe Dr., *Becoming Supernatural*, (Hay House UK), 2019

Elrod, Hal, *The Miracle Morning*,

Frankl, Victor E., *Man's Search for Meaning*, (Rider), 2004

Grant, Adam, *Originals*, (WH Allen), 2016

Hamel, Gary, *Leading the Revolution*, (Plume), 2002

Harari, Yuval Noah, *21 Lessons for the 21st Century*, (Penguin Random House), 2018

Harari, Yuval Noah, *Sapiens*, (Vintage), 2011

Hardy, Darren, *The Compound Effect*, (Hachette Books), 2020

Harry, Prince, *Spare*, (Penguin Random House), 2023

Hawking, Stephen, *A Brief History of Time*, (Bantam Books), 2011

Hemenway, Priya, *The Secret Code*, (Evergreen), 2008

Jorgenson, Eric, *The Almanack of Naval Ravikant*, (John Murray Learning). 2016

Kaufman, Josh, *The Personal MBA*, (Portfolio Penguin), 2011

Kinsley, Michael, *Creative Capitalism*, (Somon & Schuster), 2009

Maslow, Abraham, H.M., *A Theory of Human Motivation*, (Wilder Publications), 2013

Misner, Ivan, Davies, Greg & Lewis, Julian, *Infinite Giving*, (Ivan Misner), 2020

Mukherjee, Siddhartha, *The Gene: An Intimate Story*, (Magrathea), 2020

Navidad, A. E., *Simply Psychology*,

Neumann, Erich, *The Great Mother*, (Princeton), 1983

Peale, Norman Vincent, *The Power of Positive Thinking*, (Cedar Books/ Vermillion), 1990

Peterson, Jordan B., *Beyond Order -12 More Rules for Life*, (Allen Lane), 2021

Peterson, Jordan B., *Peacemaking among higher-order primates*, (Journal), 2006

Pinker, Steven, *Better Angels of our nature*, (Penguin Books), 2012

Pope, Francis, *Let us Dream -The Path to a Better Future*, (Somon & Schuster), 2020

Rhor, Richard, *The Wisdom Pattern*, (Vintage), 2016

Riemen, Rob, *To Fight Against This Age*, (W. W. Norton & Company), 2018

Rosling, Hans, Ola and Anna, *Factfulness*, (Sceptre), 2019

Rovelli, Carlo, *Reality is not what it seems*, (Penguin), 2014

Rovelli, Carlo, *Seven Brief Lessons on Physics*, (Penguin), 2014

Rovelli, Carlo, *The Order of Time (Memory)*, (Penguin), 2018

Shakespeare, William, *Macbeth* (Wordsworth), 1992

References

Sinek, Simon, *Start With Why*, (Penguin), 2011

Tzu, Sun, *The Art of War*, (Arcturus), 2018

Walsh, J., *PEST Analysis*, (Cheltaham: EBSCOhost), 2015

Websites

Admiral Joraxx, *The Father the Son and the Donkey*, (HubPages), https://discover.hubpages.com/animals/the-father-the-son-and-the-horse

Colyard, K.W., *The Ultimate Guide To The Matrix Trilogy*, (Bustle), https://www.bustle.com/entertainment/the-matrix-trilogy-summary-recap-characters

Dispenza, Joe, Dr., *Trust the Universe! The Attitide Of Gratitude* (Good Vibez), https://www.youtube.com/watch?v=LH9ybYW-wks

Duckworth, Angela Lee, *Grit: the power of passion and perseverance*, (YouTube), https://www.youtube.com/watch?v=H14bBuluwB8

Editors, The, *Biases*, (DriveTech Limited) https://www.drivetech.co.uk/ 10/5/23

Editors, The, *Sigmund Freud: the man who revolutionized Psychology with Psychoanalysis*, (Psychologistworld.com), https://www.psychologistworld.com/psychologists/sigmund-freud

Editors, The, *Repeated Quotes*, (Brainy Quote), https://www.brainyquote.com/topics/repeated-quotes

Editors, The, *Rocky Balboa Speech – 5 Life Lessons*, (Wild Child Sports), https://wildchildsports.com/rocky-balboa-speech-5-life-lessons/ 105/5/23

Hillenbrand, Philipp, Kiewell, Dieter, Miller-Cheevers, Rory, Ostojic, Ivan & Springer, Gisa, *Traditional company, new businesses: The pairing that can ensure an incumbent's survival*, (McKinsey & Company) https://www.mckinsey.com/~/media/McKinsey/Industries/Electric%20Power%20and%20Natural%20Gas/Our%20Insights/Traditional%20company%20new%20businesses%20The%20pairing%20that%20can%20ensure%20an%20incumbents%20survival/Traditional-company-new-businesses-VF.ashx

Jacobson, S., *Sigmund Freud's Main Theories in Psychoanalysis: A Quick Summary*, (Harley Therapy) https://www.harleytherapy.co.uk/counselling/freuds-main-theories-psychoanalysis.htm

Jobs, Steve, *'You've got to find what you love,' Jobs says*, (Stanford News), https://news.stanford.edu/2005/06/14/jobs-061505/

Kazan, Dick, *Abraham Lincoln: A remarkable story of perseverance*, (Kazan Today), https://www.kazantoday.com/WeeklyArticles/abraham-lincoln.html

Kelani, Tunde, *Saworoide*, https://www.youtube.com/watch?v=lqON2t9mBks

Lathrap, Mary, T., *Judge Softly or Walk a Mile in His Moccasins*, (James Milton), https://jamesmilson.com/about-the-blog/judge-softly-or-walk-a-mile-in-his-moccasins-by-mary-t-lathrap/ 10/5/23

Martin, Emmie & Loudenback, Tanza, *Insider*, (Insider), https://www.businessinsider.com/most-generous-people-in-the-world-2015-10?r=US&IR=T

Melo, Rigo, *Education is Life*, (The National), https://www.thenational.com.pg/education-is-life/ 10/5/23

Nair, Shreejit, *The Matrix Resurrections Movie Review & Summary: Resurrects Neo and Trinity to Bury Remains of the Original Trilogy*, (EnterNews), https://themovieculture.com/the-matrix-resurrections-movie-review-and-summary/

Navidad, A. E., *Marshmallow Test Experiment and Delayed Gratification*, (Simply Psychology) https://www.simplypsychology.org/marshmallow-test.html

Pathak, Indra Raj, *Thomas Edison on Perseverance*, https://medium.com/illumination/what-thomas-edison-can-teach-you-about-perseverance-3c6d05caa57d#:~:text=Outstanding%20inventor%2C%20Edison%2C%20famously%20said,didn't%20fail%201000%20times

Peterson, Jordan, *A hard truth for the Creative People*, (REDDOT X), https://www.youtube.com/watch?v=BMkCVEvfkUU

Puchko, Kristy, *15 Things You Might Not Know About Leonardo da Vinci's Vitruvian Man*, (Minute Media) https://www.mentalfloss.com/article/71390/15-things-you-might-not-know-about-leonardo-da-vincis-vitruvian-man

Roda Anubhav, *Persistent stories of success in sports*, https://blog.playo.co/10-inspiring-sports-stories-from-being-a-failure-to-success/

Schwantes, Marcel, *Warren Buffett Thinks You Should Hire for Integrity First. Here Are 5 Questions to Ask Job Candidates*, (Inc.), https://www.inc.com/marcel-schwantes/warren-buffett-thinks-you-should-hire-for-integrity-first-here-are-5-questions-to-ask-job-candidates.html

References

Unknown Author, *Don't find fault*, https://lifemostinspiringpoems.blogspot.com/2014/03/dont-find-fault-author-unknown.html

Unknown Author, *The dog hides his mother*, (All Folk Tales), http://www.allfolktales.com/wafrica/dog_hides_his_mother.php

Blooming Through Chaotic Times

ABOUT THE AUTHOR

*If you want to be an author,
the first step you need to take is just to write,
and write all the time*

Abbirose Adey

About the Author

Francis is the founder of ARC and You, an organisation dedicated to helping people find purpose in their lives through a synergy of Awareness, Relationship, and Career. Through this, Francis is able to help individuals discover their true calling and achieve their full potential.

As the CEO of ARC Facilities, Francis is devoted to creating sustainable projects within the domestic and commercial building industry, where he is able to make a significant impact on the environment, helping to promote a more sustainable future for us all. Francis is also the founder of Framat, a management consultancy company.

Francis is curator of: 'A Synergy of 3 Civilizations: The British, Yorubas & Benin (Edos)', a Royal Borough of Greenwich Funded project which consists of guided exhibitions, lectures and panel discussions which explored the cultural richness and complex historical relationship between the British, Yoruba and Benin empires. This exhibition is touring various institutions across London, including The Royal Observatory Museum.

Francis studied Engineering at the Universities of Ilorin and Lagos, Nigeria and Management at Plymouth University, UK and Education at the London School of Academics. He is a board member of the organisations SPAPTAN, NetTrust, and Framat. He is a Member of the Institute of Leadership and Management and The Institute of Workplace and Facilities Management and is regularly featured in interviews and articles.

Francis believes in the thriving of all and as such his personal slogan is 'Passionate about Living' and his motto is 'For Service and Peace'.

He was born in Oshogbo, Nigeria and now lives in London, UK. He is married to Evelyn: they have three children: Ifeoluwa, Mercy, and Maria.

INDEX

A

Adey, Abbirose iii, 287, 295
Adey, Ladey ix, xiii
Admiral Joraxx 291
African Proverb 85
African Wisdom 116
Alcoholics Anonymous 89
Alujonjonkijon Fable xiii, 117, 118, 133
Apple 170
ARC and You 33, 103, 282
Armed Forces Remembrance Day 111

B

Barnum, P T 178
Berlin, Isaiah 138
Bhaktivedanta, Swami 220, 265
Big Bang Theory 234, 235
Brexit 27
Buffett, Warren 224, 225
Burg, Bob 214

C

Cameron, David 26
Churchill, Winston 92, 115, 162, 221
Coelho, Paulo 68, 98
Columbus, Christopher 182
Colyard, K.W. 291
Covid-19 27

D

Dante, Alighieri 240, 243, 244, 245, 246
Darwin, Charles 9, 125, 126, 146
Davies, Greg 215, 290
da Vinci, Leonardo 166, 240, 241, 244, 246, 252, 292
Davis, Ray 51
Disney
  Lion King, The 281
Dispenza, Joe, Dr. 291
Duckworth, Angela Lee 79, 291

E

Ecclesiastes 275
Edison, Thomas 86
Edwards, Tryon 82
Einstein, Albert 6, 89, 137, 173, 177, 211, 229, 235
Elliot, George 110
Elrod, Hal 165

F

Framat 33, 103
Frankl, Victor 268

Freud, Sigmund 240, 241, 242, 243, 244, 246, 247, 250, 277
Fulani 41

G

Gates, Bill 224, 225
Gates, Melinda 224
General Mills 170
Ghandi, Mahatma 199
Giussani, Luigi 255
Google 170
Guest, Edgar A 92

H

Hans Rosling 147
Hillenbrand, Philipp 291
Holocaust Memorial 111
Homer
  Odysseus 99, 100, 101, 102, 103, 104, 166
  The Odyssey 99, 166

I

Ingham, Harrington 165
Innosight 168

J

Jacobson, S 291
Jefferson, Thomas 157
Jobs, Steve 49, 51, 61
Johari Window 165
Johnson, Boris 26
Jordan, Michael 85
Jung, Carl 245, 249, 268

K

Karma 67, 69
Kazan, Dick 292
Kelani, Tunde 206, 292
Keller, Helen 83
Kierkegaard, Søren 113
Kiewell, Dieter 291
King Ferdinand II 182
King, Martin Luther, Jr. 54, 55, 199, 303
Kuti, Fela Anikulapo 55

L

Lathrap, Mary T 72
Lee, Harper 197
Lewis, Julian 215, 290
Lincoln, Abraham 86, 199
Loudenback, Tanza 292
Louvre, The 193
Luft, Joseph 165

M

Mandela, Nelson 182
Mann, John David 214
Manson, Mark 82
Marshmallow Experiment of Delayed Gratification 46
Martin, Emmie 292
Maslow, Abraham 13, 223, 290
May, Theresa 26
Microsoft 224
Miller-Cheevers, Rory 291
Mischel, Walter 46
Misner, Ivan Dr 92, 153, 215, 290
Mitochondria 127
Mitochondrial Eve 128

Index

Most Recent Common Ancestor (MRCA) 128
Mother Teresa 199, 223
Mukherjee, Siddhartha 127, 290
Murphy's Law
Musk, Elon , 61

N

Nair, Shreejit 292
Navidad, A. E. 291, 292
Neumann, Erich 290
Niebuhr, Reinhold 89
Nietzsche, Friedrich 42, 89, 187

O

Optimism Bias 71
Ostojic, Ivan 291
Oyo Empire 194

P

Pathak, Indra Raj 292
Peale, Norman Vincent 290
PESTEL 33, 36, 39
Peterson, Jordan 279, 290, 292
Peters, Tom 280
Piaget, Jean 183, 266
Pinker, Steven 147, 290
Pinocchio 279
Polo, Marco 182
Prince Harry 111
Prince William 111
Puchko, Kristy 292

Q

Queen Elizabeth II 111
Queen Isabella I 182

R

Ravikant, Naval 82
Rhor, Richard 290
Riemen, Rob 290
Risk 39
Rocky 88
Roda Anubhav 292
Romer, Paul 90
Rosling, Hans, Ola and Anna 6, 147, 290
Rovelli, Carlo 290
Rumi 109

S

Salesforce 170
Saworoide 206
Schwantes, Marcel 292
Shakespeare, William 290
    Macbeth 277
Sinek, Simon 291
SMART 34, 91
Springer, Gisa 291
Standard & Poor (S&P) 168
Stanford University 49
SWOT 33, 37, 39

T

Thatcher, Margaret 216
The Matrix 222, 249, 250, 251
    The Matrix Resurrection 250
The Shawshank Redemption 52
Trump, Donald J 27
Tyson, Mike
Tzu, Sun 291

V

Vitruvian Man 240, 241, 246, 247

W

Walsh, J. 291
Winfrey, Oprah 224

Y

Yoruba xii, 152, 153, 231
Yousafzai, Malala 224

Z

Zero-sum 195

NOTES

If you want to change the world, pick up a pen and write

Martin Luther King Jr.

PLEASE USE THE following pages to note down any thoughts and questions you have about your own Journey; whether it be to help you to sustain focus, show gratitude for anything in your life or a memory to wish to hold onto. This is also a place to make help answer any of the questions from the practical suggestion after each Principle.

I have alternated the note pages between lined and blank as we all work in our unique way - you may wish to draw out some ideas without the hindrance of lines, or use a guide when writing.

Notes

Blooming Through Chaotic Times

Notes

Blooming Through Chaotic Times

Notes

Blooming Through Chaotic Times

Notes

Blooming Through Chaotic Times

Notes

Blooming Through Chaotic Times

www.ingramcontent.com/pod-product-compliance
Lightning Source LLC
Chambersburg PA
CBHW041214130526
44590CB00061BA/4023